JESUS' FAREWELL DISCOURSE

A 12-WEEK STUDY

Stephen Witmer

WHEATON, ILLINOIS

Knowing the Bible: Jesus' Farewell Discourse, A 12-Week Study

Published by Crossway
1300 Crescent Street
Wheaton, Illinois 60187

Cover design: Simplicated Studio

First printing 2025

Printed in the United States of America

All emphases in Scripture quotations have been added by the author.

Trade paperback ISBN: 978-1-4335-9947-7

EPub ISBN: 978-1-4335-9949-1
PDF ISBN: 978-1-4335-9948-4

Crossway is a publishing ministry of Good News Publishers.

VP 35 34 33 32 31 30 29 28 27 26 25
15 14 13 12 11 10 9 8 7 6 5 4 3 2 1

"This series is a tremendous resource for those wanting to study and teach the Bible with an understanding of how the gospel is woven throughout Scripture. Here are gospel-minded pastors and scholars doing gospel business from all the Scriptures. This is a biblical and theological feast preparing God's people to apply the entire Bible to all of life with heart and mind wholly committed to Christ's priorities."

BRYAN CHAPELL, pastor; author, *Christ-Centered Preaching* and *Christ-Centered Worship*

"Mark Twain may have smiled when he wrote to a friend, 'I didn't have time to write you a short letter, so I wrote you a long letter.' But the truth of Twain's remark remains serious and universal, because well-reasoned, compact writing requires extra time and extra hard work. And this is what we have in the Crossway Bible study series *Knowing the Bible*. The skilled authors and notable editors provide the contours of each book of the Bible as well as the grand theological themes that bind them together as one Book. Here, in a 12-week format, are carefully wrought studies that will ignite the mind and the heart."

R. KENT HUGHES, Senior Pastor Emeritus, College Church, Wheaton, Illinois

"*Knowing the Bible* brings together a gifted team of Bible teachers to produce a high-quality series of study guides. The coordinated focus of these materials is unique: biblical content, provocative questions, systematic theology, practical application, and the gospel story of God's grace presented all the way through Scripture."

PHILIP G. RYKEN, President, Wheaton College

"These *Knowing the Bible* volumes provide a significant and very welcome variation on the general run of inductive Bible studies. This series provides substantial instruction, as well as teaching through the very questions that are asked. *Knowing the Bible* then goes even further by showing how any given text links with the gospel, the whole Bible, and the formation of theology. I heartily endorse this orientation of individual books to the whole Bible and the gospel, and I applaud the demonstration that sound theology was not something invented later by Christians, but is right there in the pages of Scripture."

GRAEME L. GOLDSWORTHY, former lecturer in Old Testament, Biblical Theology, and Hermeneutics, Moore Theological College

"What a gift to earnest, Bible-loving, Bible-searching believers! The organization and structure of the Bible study format presented through the *Knowing the Bible* series is so well conceived. Students of the Word are led to understand the content of passages through perceptive, guided questions, and they are given rich insights and application all along the way in the brief but illuminating sections that conclude each study. What potential growth in depth and breadth of understanding these studies offer! One can only pray that vast numbers of believers will discover more of God and the beauty of his Word through these rich studies."

BRUCE A. WARE, T. Rupert and Lucille Coleman Professor of Christian Theology, The Southern Baptist Theological Seminary

KNOWING THE BIBLE

Douglas Sean O'Donnell, Series Editor

• • • • • •

Genesis
Exodus
Leviticus
Numbers
Deuteronomy
Joshua
Judges
Ruth and Esther
1–2 Samuel
1–2 Kings
1–2 Chronicles
Ezra and Nehemiah
Job
Psalms
Proverbs
Ecclesiastes
Song of Solomon
Isaiah
Jeremiah
Lamentations, Habakkuk, and Zephaniah
Ezekiel
Daniel
Hosea
Joel, Amos, and Obadiah
Jonah, Micah, and Nahum
Haggai, Zechariah, and Malachi
Matthew
Mark
Luke
John
Acts
Romans
1 Corinthians
2 Corinthians
Galatians
Ephesians
Philippians
Colossians and Philemon
1–2 Thessalonians
1–2 Timothy and Titus
Hebrews
James
1–2 Peter and Jude
1–3 John
Revelation

The Ten Commandments
The Miracles of Jesus
The Parables of Jesus
Jesus' Speech on the Mount of Olives
The Sermon on the Mount
Jesus' Farewell Discourse

• • • • • •

DOUGLAS SEAN O'DONNELL (PhD, University of Aberdeen) is the Senior Vice President of Bible Editorial at Crossway. He is the author and editor of more than a dozen books, including *The Beginning and End of Wisdom*; *The Pastor's Book*; *The Song of Solomon* and *Matthew* in the Preaching the Word commentary series; and *Psalms* and *The Parables of Jesus* in the Knowing the Bible series. He also contributed "Song of Solomon" and "Job" to the ESV Expository Commentary.

TABLE OF CONTENTS

SERIES PREFACE

KNOWING THE BIBLE, as the title indicates, was created to help readers know and understand the meaning, the message, and the God of the Bible. This series was created and edited by Lane Dennis and Dane Ortlund, and J. I. Packer served as the theological editor. Dr. Packer has gone to be with the Lord, Lane has retired as CEO and president of Crossway, and Dane now serves as senior pastor of Naperville (Illinois) Presbyterian Church. We are so grateful for their labors in overseeing the first forty-plus volumes of this series! To honor and expand upon their idea, we are continuing the series, focusing on key sections from Scripture, such as the Ten Commandments and the Sermon on the Mount.

Each volume in the series consists of twelve units that progressively take the reader through a clear, concise, and deep study of certain portions of Scripture. The material works best for a small group, as the questions are designed for good interactive group discussion. Even so, an individual could easily use the material for a personal Bible study as well.

Week 1 provides an overview of the section or sections of Scripture to be studied, which includes placing the text into its larger context (e.g., the Sermon on the Mount within the Gospel of Matthew), providing key historical background, and offering some questions to get started. Weeks 2–12 each have the following features: a summary of how the text fits into the rest of Scripture ("The Place of the Passage"), a summary sentence on the main theme ("The Big Picture"), and ten or so questions ("Reflection and Discussion Questions"). Moreover, each unit highlights the role of the gospel of grace in each text ("Gospel Glimpses"), identifies whole-Bible themes ("Whole-Bible Connections"), pinpoints Christian doctrines ("Theological Soundings"), defines key terms ("Definitions"), and allows space to respond ("Personal Implications").

Lastly, to help readers understand the Bible better, we urge readers to use the ESV Bible and the *ESV Study Bible*, which are available in various print and digital formats, including online editions at esv.org. The *Knowing the Bible* series is also available online.

May our gracious God, who has generously given his Spirit and his Word, use this study to grow his people in their knowledge and love of the Father, Son, and Spirit.

Douglas Sean O'Donnell
Series Editor

WEEK 1: OVERVIEW

Getting Acquainted

John 13–17 is a remarkable and precious portion of Scripture. In these chapters Jesus washes the feet of his disciples (John 13), prepares them for his imminent departure and their future mission (John 14–16), and prays to the Father in the longest of all Jesus' prayers recorded in the Bible (John 17). Chapters 13–17 contain numerous words and actions of Jesus not mentioned in the other Gospels, including Jesus' washing of his disciples' feet; his claim to be the way, the truth, and the life; his famous image of the vine and the branches; and his remarkable prayer to the Father. Everything Jesus says and does in John 13–17 is motivated by his exceeding love for his disciples (John 13:1) and is loaded with extra significance because these events occur the night before his crucifixion.

As we approach our study of John 13–17, it is important to be aware that, in order to read John's Gospel as John intends, we cannot hold it at arm's length, treating it as merely a set of facts or an interesting historical document. Rather we must receive it personally. This is clear in John 20:30–31, where John announces the purpose of his writing: "Jesus did many other signs in the presence of the disciples, which are not written in this book; but these are written so that you may believe that Jesus is the Christ, the Son of God, and that by believing you may have life in his name." The word "you" in verse 31 addresses readers—including us! John means to awaken and sustain our faith so that we may have spiritual life. To read John's Gospel the way a scholar studies an archival document about rental rates in New York City in the 1850s is to miss the point.

That yellowed document was never addressed to us. But this gospel is. So we are meant to read it as we would read a letter from our landlord telling us he will give us the apartment we have been renting if we are willing to receive it. It is ours for free if we will have it!

Placing It in the Larger Story

John's Gospel comprises two main sections: Jesus' public ministry of signs[1] in John 1–12 (often called the Book of Signs) and the manifestation of Jesus' glory, culminating at the cross, in John 13–21 (often called the Book of Glory). John 13–17 thus comes at a pivotal point in the Gospel, as Jesus turns from his public ministry to a private one, preparing the group of disciples for his imminent death and departure and their subsequent mission to the world.

John 13–17 also forms a crucial pause in the external action of John's Gospel, falling as it does between the ministry activity of John 1–12 and the climactic trial, crucifixion, and resurrection in John 18–21. By contrast John 13–17 contains far fewer actions than words—in these chapters, Jesus teaches and Jesus prays. Importantly, this pause allows the first disciples (and also subsequent readers of the Gospel) to reflect on what has come before and to prepare for the climactic events soon to occur.

Key Verse

"Now before the Feast of the Passover, when Jesus knew that his hour had come to depart out of this world to the Father, having loved his own who were in the world, he loved them to the end" (John 13:1).

Date and Historical Background

Although there have been many guesses as to who wrote the Gospel of John, the most likely candidate is John, the son of Zebedee, likely the one referred to several times in this Gospel as the "disciple whom Jesus loved." Internal and external evidence suggests that John probably wrote the Gospel between AD 70 and 100 (see *ESV Study Bible*, pages 2015–2017).

Occurring soon after Jesus' triumphal entry[2] into Jerusalem (John 12:12–19), the events of John 13–17 take place on the Thursday night of the Passover meal (which is explicitly recounted in the other Gospels, but which in John receives only a mention in 13:1). Just before Jesus eats the meal with his disciples, he washes their feet. Good Friday—the day of Jesus' crucifixion—is tomorrow.

Outline of John 13–17

I. **Jesus Loved Them to the End (13:1–20)**
II. **Jesus and Judas (13:21–30)**
III. **A New Commandment (13:31–38)**
IV. **The Expression, Evidence, and Outcome of Jesus' Love (14:1–31)**
V. **Abiding in the Vine (15:1–17)**
VI. **Hated by the World, Part 1 (15:18–27)**
VII. **Hated by the World, Part 2 (16:1–15)**
VIII. **A Call to Courage (16:16–33)**
IX. **The Prayer of Jesus (17:1–26)**

As You Get Started

Have you previously studied John 13–17 on your own or as part of a small group or Sunday school class? Has your pastor ever preached on these chapters? From your previous experience with John 13–17, what knowledge or questions do you bring to this current study?

Skim through John 13–17 and note any questions that arise. Jot these down to revisit throughout the course of this study.

Imagine that somehow you know for certain that you will die tomorrow. With whom will you choose to spend your few remaining hours? What will you say to or do with them? Having considered your own response, now read John 13–17 with a view toward seeing Jesus' response in that same situation. What does this tell us about Jesus?

As You Finish This Unit . . .

Take a moment now to ask for the Lord's blessing and help as you continue in this study of John 13–17. Take a moment also to look back through this unit of study, to reflect on some key things that the Lord may be teaching you, and perhaps to highlight and underline these things to review in the future.

Definitions

[1] **Signs** – In John's Gospel, Jesus' miracles are referred to as "signs." They are understood not mainly as wonderful acts of power but as pointers to the identity of Jesus himself. John's Gospel contains seven signs recorded in John 1–12, climaxing with the raising of Lazarus in John 11.

[2] **Triumphal entry** – Jesus' entrance into Jerusalem on a donkey and to popular acclaim from the crowds, with shouts of "Hosanna!" This event is recorded in all four Gospels.

Week 2: Jesus Loved Them to the End

John 13:1–20

The Place of the Passage

John 13:1–20 is crucially important for understanding all that will follow in chapters 13–17 (as well as in the remainder of John's Gospel). The emphasis on Jesus' knowledge demonstrates that he is in full control of unfolding events, including his own death. Additionally, the focus on Jesus' love—including the full significance of the foot washing—shows that Jesus' coming speech, prayer, and death are expressions of love for his disciples. Jesus will, in turn, form a *community* of those who love one another as he has loved them (13:15).

The Big Picture

Jesus knows his death is imminent and will lead to his return to the Father. In this knowledge, and with full love for the new community he is creating, he prepares his disciples beforehand for his departure and for their future life together.

Reflection and Discussion

Read through the complete passage for this study, John 13:1–20. Then review the following questions and record your responses. (For further background, see the *ESV Study Bible*, pages 2050–2051, or visit esv.org.)

John 13:1 frames everything that Jesus does in John 13–17 as being motivated by his overwhelming love ("to the end") for his disciples. How specifically do we see Jesus' love displayed in this passage?

What particular facets of Jesus' knowledge does John choose to highlight in verses 1–20 (e.g., 13:1, 11)? In what ways does Jesus' comprehensive knowledge motivate his actions?

To see how John 13:1–20 (and John 13–17 as a whole) functions as a pivot point in the Gospel, identify the references in this passage both to Jesus' past and to Jesus' future. Where in this passage is Jesus' knowledge of his imminent death mentioned (see also 13:33; 14:29; 16:28)?

John's Gospel uses the phrase "his own" (13:1) also in John 1:1–18. To what does this phrase refer in John 1? In John 13:1? What is the significance of its being used both at the beginning of Jesus' public ministry and here at the beginning of his private ministry to the disciples?

In what way does John communicate the full responsibility of Judas for his own actions (13:11; cf. 6:66–71; 12:4; 18:1–5)? How does he show the involvement of the devil, or Satan,[1] in what Judas is doing (13:2, cf. 13:27)? How does he demonstrate that even the culpable actions of Judas and the evil plans of Satan are ultimately within the sovereign plan of God (13:18) and are known fully by Jesus (13:11, 19)?

Notice in verses 2–4 the elaborate introduction to Jesus' actions. The main verb of the sentence is "rose," which does not appear until verse 4! How does this long buildup inform what Jesus does? How does it emphasize the importance of the foot washing? Notice also that every little detail of Jesus' actions is recounted in verses 4–5: he rose, laid aside his outer garments, took a towel, tied it around his waist, poured water into a basin, and the like. Why does John slow down so dramatically at this point in his telling of the story?

Jesus' exchange with Simon Peter in verses 6–11 may seem confusing. Why does Peter refuse Jesus so vehemently? Why does Jesus insist on washing Peter's feet?

Some church traditions practice foot washing in their worship services in light of Jesus' words in John 13:14–15. Does your tradition do this? Do you think faithfulness to Jesus' words requires literal foot washing? Are there other viable ways to obey the spirit of Jesus' example and instruction?

Have there been situations in your life in which someone of higher status has served you in a humble way? How did you feel in that situation? If you have not experienced this, use your imagination: consider how you would feel if your pastor or boss came to your house and spent ten minutes cleaning your toilet. What would be going through your mind and heart?

According to Jesus' words to the disciples in verses 12–17, why did he wash their feet? How does he intend his actions to shape the new community he is creating? According to verse 17, what will be the result for those who follow through on Jesus' purpose?

Jesus' words in verse 20 are delivered with emphasis ("Truly, truly, I say to you"). How do they fit with what he says up to this point in 13:1–20, and why does he emphasize them so strongly?

Read through the following three sections on *Gospel Glimpses*, *Whole-Bible Connections*, and *Theological Soundings*. Then take time to consider the *Personal Implications* these sections have for you.

Gospel Glimpses

THE HOUR HAS COME. Jesus' "hour"[2] is mentioned throughout John's Gospel and refers to the time of his death on the cross. We are told repeatedly in the first half of the Gospel that it has not yet come. For instance, at the wedding feast in Cana Jesus tells his mother, "My hour has not yet come" (John 2:4; cf. 7:6–8, 30; 8:20). However, beginning in John 12 we see a dramatic change. Just after the coming of the Greeks in 12:20–22, Jesus announces, "The hour has come for the Son of Man to be glorified" (12:23) and "For this purpose I have come to this hour" (12:27). In John 13:1 we are told that "Jesus knew that his hour had come to depart out of this world to the Father." Clearly in John's Gospel Jesus' death is not a random incident, an accident, or an afterthought. Rather, the Gospel points to it from the very beginning, for it is at the heart of what Jesus came to do. As John the Baptist says at the beginning of Jesus' ministry (likely speaking better than he knows), "Behold, the Lamb of God, who takes away the sin of the world!" (1:29). Jesus' death is of central importance.

JESUS' LOVE "TO THE END." John 13:1 remarks, "Having loved his own who were in the world, he loved them to the end." The expression "to the end" can mean two things. As a temporal phrase it would mean, "He loved them all the way until the end of his life." As an intensive phrase it would mean, "He loved them to the uttermost" or "fully." In this context it probably means both. Jesus loved his disciples as long as he could, and he loved them as much as anyone could. Consider this remarkable love of our Savior. On the eve of his own death, aware of personal betrayal from an intimate companion, at a time when other people would naturally rely on support from those around them, Jesus reaches out in love to his followers to the end and to the uttermost.

THE FOOT WASHING. It is difficult for us to understand at our cultural distance just how shocking the foot washing would be. In Jesus' time and culture washing dirty feet was a menial, undesirable task. Non-Jewish slaves did it. Very rarely, peers of equal status might wash one another's feet, and only when they wanted to express great love. Never would someone of higher status wash the feet of a lower-status person. But that is what Jesus does. John narrates it in minute detail to emphasize its importance. And the shock value of this symbolic action is entirely appropriate, because it in fact symbolizes something far more shocking. Jesus will cleanse his disciples from their sins through his agonizing death on a Roman cross. By symbolically previewing his sin-cleansing death (13:8) Jesus grants his disciples an embodied experience of the meaning of the cross before it happens. They *see* his humble kneeling. They *feel* his hands scouring grime from their feet. They *hear* the water as it splashes into the basin. When they wonder later whether they really are forgiven, they will recall their experience in this moment and know the love of their Savior.

Whole-Bible Connections

HIS OWN. We are told in 13:1 that, "having loved his own who were in the world, [Jesus] loved them to the end." In context "his own" refers clearly to his disciples (13:5). But to understand the full significance of that little phrase it is important to see how it is used at the beginning of John's Gospel. John 1:11 says that Jesus "came to his own, and his own people did not receive him." There "his own" refers to the Jewish people. Unfortunately, throughout John 1–12 Jesus' public ministry of signs is largely rejected by the Jewish people. So, in a stunning turn in John 12, Jesus responds to this unbelief by withdrawing from his public ministry of signs and hiding himself (12:36–37). It is no coincidence that, after Jesus has withdrawn from his public ministry to prepare his disciples for his coming death, the phrase "his own" is repurposed and applied to them. "His own" in 13:1 refers not to an ethnic people but to his disciples, those who belong to him through faith, a messianic community that will include both Jews and Gentiles. Jesus is creating for himself a new people, a new family (cf. 1:12–13; 20:17).

JUDAS'S DEPARTURE AND BETRAYAL. Importantly, Judas's betrayal was foretold by God through the Scriptures. Jesus demonstrates this by identifying Judas's betrayal as the fulfillment of Psalm 41:9, which refers to Absalom's rebellion against his father, King David. Additionally, Judas's betrayal was foreknown by Jesus himself (cf. John 6:64, 70–71). Jesus' knowledge of Judas demonstrates Jesus' surpassing greatness; he predicts the betrayal to his disciples so that, when it happens, they will believe that "I am," which elsewhere in John has clear overtones of God's self-identification as "I AM WHO I AM" (Ex. 3:14; cf. John 8:58).

Theological Soundings

JESUS' PREEXISTENCE. John's Gospel is clear that Jesus' birth was not the beginning of his existence. Rather, from eternity he was always in perfect fellowship with the Father (John 1:1–4, 18; 8:58; 17:24). In John 13:3–4 we see that Jesus' assurance of his fellowship with God (from eternity past and into eternity future) motivates his love for his disciples: "Jesus, knowing that the Father had given all things into his hands, and that he had come from God and was going back to God, rose from supper." Jesus' utter confidence in his perfect fellowship with God the Father is the basis of his loving action for his own. In other words Jesus' preexistence is not mere abstract theological truth; it is the basis of our salvation.

HEARING JOHN 13–17 TODAY. As we have seen, John 20:30–31 demonstrates that, as readers of John's Gospel, we are personally involved. And yet we must also recognize that Jesus' words and actions in John 13–17 apply first to the original disciples and then secondarily to us. In fact these chapters are applicable to us precisely *because* they apply first to the original disciples. John 13–17 explains how it is that remarkable gospel progress comes from the horrible circumstances of John 18–19. Jesus prepares his disciples beforehand and promises them his own resurrected presence and the coming of the Holy Spirit. As future disciples, we appear briefly in John 17:20–26, where Jesus prays for those who will believe through the "word" of the first disciples. Of course, we could not believe if the disciples had not spoken the gospel word. John 13–17 explains how it is that they spoke even after the crushing events of John 18–19.

Personal Implications

Take time to reflect on the implications of John 13:1–20 for your own life today. Make notes below on the personal implications for your walk with the Lord of (1) the *Gospel Glimpses*, (2) the *Whole-Bible Connections*, (3) the *Theological Soundings*, and (4) this passage as a whole.

1. Gospel Glimpses

2. Whole-Bible Connections

3. Theological Soundings

4. John 13:1–20

As You Finish This Unit . . .

Take a moment now to ask for the Lord's blessing and help as you continue in this study of John 13–17. Take a moment also to look back through this unit of study, to reflect on some key things that the Lord may be teaching you, and perhaps to highlight and underline these things to review in the future.

Definitions

[1] **Satan** – In John 13 "the devil" (13:2) and "Satan" (13:27) refer to the real, personal, incorporeal, spiritual enemy of God.

[2] **Hour** – In John's Gospel the term "hour" refers not to a sixty-minute length of time but rather more generally to the period of time in which something occurs—especially Jesus' betrayal, suffering, and death.

WEEK 3: JESUS AND JUDAS

John 13:21–30

The Place of the Passage

John 13:21–30 continues the account of Jesus' final night with his disciples, which began in 13:1–20. Now the Gospel writer focuses our attention on Judas's betrayal of Jesus. We have already seen Judas's culpable responsibility for the betrayal (13:11), together with the devil's involvement (13:2), God's overarching plan (13:18), and Jesus' full knowledge (13:19). In verses 21–30 we are shown that Jesus is in full control of all that will happen and is in fact the one moving events toward his own death.

The Big Picture

This passage demonstrates Jesus' full control of the events leading to his death.

Reflection and Discussion

Read through the complete passage for this study, John 13:21–30. Then review the following questions and record your responses. (For further background, see the *ESV Study Bible*, page 2051, or visit esv.org.)

We have seen that John 13:1 frames everything that Jesus does in John 13–17 as being motivated by his overwhelming love ("to the end") for his disciples. How do we see Jesus' love displayed specifically in 13:21–30?

What causes Jesus to be troubled (13:21)? What exactly do you think it means for Jesus to be "troubled in his spirit"? Can you think of other times in John's Gospel that Jesus is troubled (cf. 11:33; 12:27)?

How is the seriousness of Jesus' announcement about his betrayer (13:21) emphasized both by the Gospel writer and by Jesus himself? Why do you think John tells us that Jesus "testified" about this?

Imagine yourself as one of the disciples, hearing that one of your closest companions will betray Jesus. How would you feel? What would you do? Would it affect your interactions with the rest of the group? How so? How do the disciples in fact respond (13:22)?

What do we know about Judas from John's Gospel up to this point? Recall that in 6:70–71 Jesus tells his disciples that "one of you is a devil" and John immediately informs us that Jesus is speaking of "Judas the son of Simon Iscariot, for he, one of the twelve, was going to betray him." We are also told in 12:4–6 that Judas was about to betray Jesus and that he was a thief, stealing from the moneybag of which he had charge. Why do you think Jesus allowed Judas to remain among the disciples, given that Jesus knew these things about him? What would it have been like for Jesus to wash Judas's feet?

Why do you think Jesus identifies Judas as his betrayer in the particular way he does? Why does Jesus not explicitly declare to the disciples that Judas is the one?

Given that Jesus says the betrayer is the one to whom he gives the morsel of bread, and that he then gives the morsel to Judas, saying, "What you are going to do, do quickly," why does no one else at the table understand why Jesus speaks these words to Judas (13:28)? Why do they guess other possibilities (13:29)?

Why do you think John mentions in verse 30 that "it was night"?

Read through the following three sections on *Gospel Glimpses*, *Whole-Bible Connections*, and *Theological Soundings*. Then take time to consider the *Personal Implications* these sections have for you.

Gospel Glimpses

IN THE BOSOM. We are told in 13:23 that the disciple whom Jesus loved—John, the son of Zebedee, the writer of John's Gospel—"was reclining at table at Jesus' side." This Greek clause could also be rendered "Was reclining in the bosom of Jesus." In Jesus' day people at special feasts would recline at a low table while eating, with their heads resting on an elbow near the table and their feet pointing away. To recline with one's head near the chest of another guest ("in the bosom of") was to enjoy a place of favor and intimacy. That is where John is, with his head near Jesus' chest. This explains an otherwise mystifying aspect of the passage. Given that Jesus says the betrayer is the one to whom he gives a morsel of bread, why do the disciples not understand that Judas is the betrayer after Jesus hands him the morsel? It is because Jesus speaks the words of verse 26 ("It is he to whom I will give this morsel of bread when I have dipped it") only to John, in whispered tones. Only John can hear Jesus, since he is lying in the place of access and intimacy. Jesus then says to Judas, in the hearing of all the disciples, "What you are going to do, do quickly" (13:27). Because the other disciples have not heard what Jesus has said to John, they misinterpret Jesus' words (13:28–29). We see here Jesus' care for John, the disciple whom he loved.

JESUS REVEALS GOD; JOHN'S GOSPEL REVEALS JESUS. The Greek word *kolpos* ("bosom") is used only two times in John's Gospel: here in 13:23 and at John 1:18, which says, "No one has ever seen God; God the only Son, who is at the Father's side [i.e., in his bosom], he has made him known." The word for "made him known" means to explain something fully and carefully. Only Jesus can explain God the Father, because Jesus is "God the only Son" (1:18); only Jesus is "in the bosom of the Father," enjoying the special place of love and intimacy (cf. John 17:24). We can learn about God through creation and through his self-revelation in the Old Testament. But John tells us that the supreme way to know God is through Jesus. Jesus is the Word (1:1–2), the light (1:4–5, 9; 8:12), the Son (5:18–29), the glory of God that has tabernacled among us (John 1:14). He is God (1:1, 18; 20:28) and makes God known. The connection between 1:18 and 13:23 should lead readers to realize that God reveals himself uniquely through Jesus, who then reveals himself uniquely through the beloved disciple. Thus the chain of revelation goes from God to Jesus to John to John's Gospel to the readers of the Gospel, all that we may know God and have eternal life through his Son.

Whole-Bible Connections

GOD KNOWS ALL THINGS. In the Old Testament the exhaustive knowledge and sovereignty[1] of God separates him from the false gods of the nations. "I am God, and there is no other; I am God, and there is none like me, declaring the end from the beginning and from ancient times things not yet done, saying, 'My counsel shall stand, and I will accomplish all my purpose'" (Isa. 46:9–10). In John 13:21–30 Jesus knows with depth and clarity all that is about to happen to him. But, because of the secret way in which Jesus identifies Judas (conveying only to John his knowledge that Judas is the betrayer), his disciples do not yet know just how much Jesus knows. So these verses are like a time capsule, to be opened only later. Because John recorded Jesus' private words in his Gospel, later readers (including us) know that Jesus knew beforehand. Our reading of verse 26 opens the time capsule. And of course it is very important for the first disciples to realize that Jesus has known all along. In the days after his crucifixion, that awareness will reassure them that Jesus was not taken by surprise, that his death was not an accident or a mistake, that he went to it knowingly. More than that, Jesus' foreknowledge will demonstrate that he is God. Recall Jesus' words in 13:19: "I am telling you this now, before it takes place, that when it does take place you may believe that I am he."

THE ACTIVITY OF SATAN. Satan, the personal, spiritual adversary of God, is mentioned and described in both the Old and the New Testament. Among other activities he incites King David to take a census (1 Chron. 21:1), strikes Job with physical afflictions (Job 2:7), tempts Jesus in the wilderness (Matthew 4), disrupts the impact of the gospel word in the hearts of hearers (Mark 4:15), inclines Ananias to lie to the Holy Spirit (Acts 5:3), and hinders the travel plans of the apostle Paul (1 Thess. 2:18). Satan's activity in John 13 is in keeping with what we learn of him throughout the rest of the Bible. In verse 2 (where he is referred to as the devil) he puts it into the heart of Judas Iscariot to betray Jesus. In verse 27 he himself "enters into Judas." However, although Satan is involved in directing Judas's actions, it is important to notice that in this passage Judas obeys the command of Jesus (13:27, 30). We see elsewhere in Scripture (e.g. Job 1:12; 2:6) that Satan is subject ultimately to the command of God. Here too Jesus' command prevails.

NIGHT. In the Bible darkness often symbolizes the forces of chaos and evil. God's light represents truth, order, beauty, and salvation. This is particularly true in John's Gospel, which repeatedly uses the symbolism of darkness and light (e.g., John 1; 3; 8). It is not a coincidence, therefore, that, just after Judas leaves to betray Jesus, John notes that "it was night" (13:30). We are meant to feel the forces of evil as they gather around.

Theological Soundings

JESUS IS IN CONTROL. Jesus' dipping of the morsel of bread and giving it to Judas are important for two reasons. First, they fulfill Psalm 41:9, which Jesus cites in John 13:18: "He who ate my bread has lifted his heel against me." Jesus acts in accordance with the Scriptures. Second, after giving Judas the morsel, Jesus tells him, "What you are going to do, do quickly" (13:27). Accordingly, "after receiving the morsel of bread, [Judas] immediately went out" (13:30). Jesus is the one who sets in motion the events leading to his death. Jesus issues a command to Judas ("do quickly" is a Greek imperative)—not the other way around. We should recall John 10:17–18, which are key verses in John's Gospel: "For this reason the Father loves me, because I lay down my life that I may take it up again. No one takes it from me, but I lay it down of my own accord. I have authority to lay it down, and I have authority to take it up again. This charge I have received from my Father." While it is true that Judas sinfully betrays Jesus (13:30) and that Satan is active in the betrayal (13:2, 27), ultimately Jesus is in control, laying down his own life. This should increase our appreciation of Jesus' overwhelming love for his disciples (13:1). The cross is in fact his will. He is in full control.

JESUS' EMOTIONS. As we have seen, Jesus knows and controls the events leading to his death. We might therefore think he would be impassive as he moves toward the cross. But that is emphatically not the case. Verse 21 tells us that Jesus "was troubled in his spirit." The same word *troubled* is used earlier to describe Jesus' emotion as he stood outside the tomb of his friend Lazarus: "He was deeply moved in his spirit and greatly troubled" (11:33, cf. 12:27). The word refers to being shaken or stirred up. Jesus' emotions in John 11 (possibly anger) may have been directed at the lack of faith of those mourning Lazarus or at the power of death. Surely some of Jesus' feeling here in John 14 is due to his own imminent death. But John emphasizes in verse 21 how Judas's betrayal troubles Jesus. It troubles him "in his spirit," at the core of who he is. This provides us with a deeper, richer understanding of Jesus, the God-man, as he goes to his death. He is not an emotionless automaton. He knows all, he is in full control, *and* he feels it very deeply. He goes to his death not because it is easy but because he loves his people (13:1).

Personal Implications

Take time to reflect on the implications of John 13:21–30 for your own life today. Make notes below on the personal implications for your walk with the Lord of (1) the *Gospel Glimpses*, (2) the *Whole-Bible Connections*, (3) the *Theological Soundings*, and (4) this passage as a whole.

1. Gospel Glimpses

2. Whole-Bible Connections

3. Theological Soundings

4. John 13:21–30

As You Finish This Unit . . .

Take a moment now to ask for the Lord's blessing and help as you continue in this study of John 13–17. Take a moment also to look back through this unit of study, to reflect on some key things that the Lord may be teaching you, and perhaps to highlight and underline these things to review in the future.

Definitions

[1] **Sovereignty** – God's control over all things.

WEEK 4: A NEW COMMANDMENT

John 13:31–38

The Place of the Passage

After washing his disciples' feet Jesus spoke of their need for cleansing (John 13:10). Now that he has cleansed the group by sending Judas to do his vile work (13:27), Jesus begins his discourse (13:31–16:33), followed by a prayer (17:1–26), all serving as a powerful expression of his overwhelming love for the community he is creating (13:1).

The Big Picture

As Jesus nears the hour of his glorification at the cross, he prepares the disciples for his imminent absence by issuing them a commandment to love one another and by foretelling Peter's threefold denial.

Reflection and Discussion

Read through the complete passage for this study, John 13:31–38. Then review the following questions and record your responses. (For further background, see the *ESV Study Bible*, pages 2051–2052, or visit esv.org.)

We have seen that John 13:1 frames everything Jesus does in John 13–17 as being motivated by his overwhelming love ("to the end") for his disciples. How do we see Jesus' love displayed specifically in verses 31–38?

After Judas leaves, Jesus speaks (13:31). Why do you think Jesus waits until after Judas's departure to begin his Farewell Discourse?

What does Jesus mean when he says in verse 31 that the Son of Man is now glorified and that God is glorified in him? What has happened in order to bring this about "now"? Why does Jesus speak of his imminent death as the time when he will be "glorified"?

Why does Jesus refer to his disciples in verse 33 as "little children"? Note that he uses a similar expression (though a different Greek word) in 21:5. What is he communicating through this way of addressing the disciples? How does that emphasis fit within the larger purpose of John 13–17?

What does Jesus mean when he tells his disciples, "Where I am going you cannot come" (13:33)? Why will they be unable to follow him to his destination? How might his words make the disciples feel?

In Jesus' divine nature he is present at all times and in all places (cf. Matt. 18:20; 28:20). But in his human nature, immediately after his death (and then again after his ascension) he will not be present with his disciples in a physical body (John 13:33). There will be a real absence, and that absence is the main focus of John 14–16, which deals with Jesus' departure, together with his instructions and encouragement for his disciples in light of it. As a follower of Jesus today, how do you experience his constant presence with you? How do you experience his absence? What tension do you feel between these experiences of presence and absence? How does this fuel your hope for the future new creation?

Just after announcing his departure and the imminent separation that will occur between himself and his disciples, Jesus issues them a new commandment (13:34). He urges them to live out this commandment while he is away.

Though the command to love others is in fact a very old one (e.g., Lev. 19:18), in what sense is Jesus' command to "love one another" a new commandment?

What do you think Jesus means when he says that Peter will not follow him now but will follow afterward (13:36)?

Can you spot the ironies in the exchange between Jesus and Peter? What are they?

Read through the following three sections on *Gospel Glimpses*, *Whole-Bible Connections*, and *Theological Soundings*. Then take time to consider the *Personal Implications* these sections have for you.

Gospel Glimpses

WHO WILL DIE FOR WHOM? In verse 36 Simon Peter ignores what Jesus has just said in verses 34–35 and jumps back to the thing that worries him most, namely, Jesus' words in verse 33: "Where I am going you cannot come." Simon wants to know where Jesus is going. Jesus repeats himself, clarifying this time that Peter cannot follow him *now* but will follow him *later* (13:36).

Peter responds that he will lay down his life for Jesus (13:37). John always has a keen eye for irony, and he means for us to see two ironic truths in this exchange. First, Peter will in fact *not* be willing to lay down his life for Jesus, at least in the immediate future. In verse 38 Jesus predicts Peter's threefold denial, solemnly introducing his prediction with the formula "Truly, truly," which underlines the certainty of his knowledge. Second, more heartbreakingly and also more beautifully, it will in fact be *Jesus* who will die for *Peter*. Jesus will lay down his life for the sheep (10:11). Eventually, after Jesus has forgiven and restored Peter (compare the threefold denial predicted in 13:38 with the threefold restoration of Peter in 21:15–17), Peter will have the courage to glorify God through his death (21:18–19). Tender, restoring gospel love permeates Jesus' words to Peter in 13:36–38. Jesus embodies and exemplifies the very love he has commanded his disciples to show one another (13:34–35).

THE NEWNESS OF THE LOVE COMMAND. Jesus says in 13:34 that his command to love one another is a *new* command. But God commanded his people in the Old Testament to love others. The law of Moses said, "Love your neighbor as yourself" (Lev. 19:18). Jesus himself once said that all the Law and the Prophets depend on the commandments to love God and to love our neighbor as ourselves (see Matt. 22:37–40). So in what sense is Jesus' command new? It is new, among other reasons, because Jesus' followers now have a perfect example of love to follow ("Just as I have loved you," John 13:34). Moreover, Jesus' death secures forgiveness for sin and the presence of God's empowering Spirit, who enables God's people to love and forgive one another in a new way. God's people can therefore love like never before. This really is a new kind of love.

Whole-Bible Connections

A FAREWELL DISCOURSE. John 13:31–16:33 is often referred to as Jesus' Farewell Discourse. The farewell discourse is a common genre[1] throughout the Bible (see Joshua 23–24; 1 Samuel 12; 1 Kings 2:1–12; Luke 22:14–38; Acts 20:17–38). In Genesis 49 Jacob says goodbye to his sons, and in Deuteronomy 31–33 Moses does the same to Israel. Typical features of farewell discourses include predictions of death and departure, predictions of future challenges for those being left behind, provision for those who remain, encouragements to moral behavior, and a closing blessing. All these features appear in John 13:31–16:33. But we also see key differences between Jesus' Farewell Discourse and other examples. Uniquely, Jesus' farewell is only temporary, since he will soon rise from the dead and return to his disciples. He will also be present with his disciples through the Holy Spirit. Therefore Jesus' farewell is more hopeful than other examples of the genre.

NOW IS THE SON OF MAN GLORIFIED. In 13:31–32 Judas's departure leads Jesus to declare, "Now is the Son of Man[2] glorified, and God is glorified in him. If God is glorified in him, God will also glorify him in himself, and glorify him at once." This is because Judas's departure to betray Jesus sets decisively in motion the events leading to Jesus' death, and Jesus understands his death to be the moment of his glorification. Because his death is imminent and certain he can say, "*Now* is the Son of Man glorified." Jesus' exaltation is sometimes understood as occurring *after* his crucifixion, which is not wrong (cf. Phil. 2:5–11). But John's Gospel expresses a complementary and surprising perspective: Jesus' death *is* his glorification (John 12:23, 27–28) and his "lifting up" (12:32–33). The theme of glory brackets the entire Farewell Discourse, appearing both here in 13:31–32 and also in Jesus' prayer: "Now, Father, glorify me in your own presence with the glory that I had with you before the world existed" (17:5); "Father, I desire that they also, whom you have given me, may be with me where I am, to see my glory that you have given me because you loved me before the foundation of the world" (17:24).

ISAIAH'S BACKGROUND TO JESUS' GLORIFICATION. John's references to Jesus' death as his "glorification" (13:31–32) and "lifting up" (12:32) are influenced by the prophet Isaiah. In Isaiah 6:1 the prophet Isaiah sees the Lord on his throne, "high and lifted up" (cf. Isa. 57:15), and the whole earth is full of his "glory" (Isa. 6:3). In Isaiah 52:13 the servant is "high and lifted up" and "exalted." The implication is that the servant is exalted to the heavenly throne of God himself. Reading the prophet Isaiah, John puts these two passages in Isaiah together. That is why in John 12:41 he notes (stunningly!) that, when Isaiah saw God on his throne in Isaiah 6, he in fact saw Jesus, the suffering servant ("[Isaiah] saw his glory and spoke of him"). Additionally, when Jesus says in John 12:32 that he will be "lifted up from the earth," not only is he referring to his death (12:33), but for those with ears to hear he is also claiming that his death will be his exaltation to the glorious throne of God himself. Here is a spectacular and paradoxical truth right at the heart of Christianity, namely, Jesus' death on the cross is simultaneously the moment of his greatest agony and of his greatest exaltation. His death is both a literal "lifting up" to hang naked (or wearing only a loincloth) and publicly shamed on a cross and also simultaneously a manifestation of the incomparable glory of the sovereign, exalted God.

Theological Soundings

THE LOVE COMMANDMENT. Verses 34–35 are the main point of John 13:31–35, and they show Jesus' instruction for what his disciples are to do during his absence: imitate him ("Just as I have loved you") by loving one another. The importance of the love commandment is emphasized by its placement here at the beginning of Jesus' lengthy discourse in 13:31–16:33 (Jesus will return to the love commandment in 15:12, 17). The *purpose* of the love commandment is highlighted in verse 35: It is through their love for one another that all people will know these are Jesus' disciples. This introduces the theme of mission, which will be important throughout John 13–17. In his absence Jesus' disciples are not to adopt a reclusive, defensive crouch. Rather, they are sent by him and empowered by the Holy Spirit to continue the mission the Father sent Jesus himself to do (20:21–22). Gospel love for one another is one of the most effective means of gospel mission to the world.

Personal Implications

Take time to reflect on the implications of John 13:31–38 for your own life today. Make notes below on the personal implications for your walk with the Lord of (1) the *Gospel Glimpses*, (2) the *Whole-Bible Connections*, (3) the *Theological Soundings*, and (4) this passage as a whole.

1. Gospel Glimpses

2. Whole-Bible Connections

3. Theological Soundings

4. John 13:31–38

As You Finish This Unit . . .

Take a moment now to ask for the Lord's blessing and help as you continue in this study of John 13–17. Take a moment also to look back through this unit of study, to reflect on some key things that the Lord may be teaching you, and perhaps to highlight and underline these things to review in the future.

Definitions

[1] **Genre** – A type of literary work characterized by a particular style, form, and content.

[2] **Son of Man** – Jesus' favorite way of referring to himself, both in the Synoptic Gospels (Matthew, Mark, Luke) and in John's Gospel, referencing the glorious Son of Man in Daniel 7.

Week 5: The Expression, Evidence, and Outcome of Jesus' Love

John 14:1–31

The Place of the Passage

Already in John 13 we have seen that Jesus, moved by love for his disciples, tells them of his impending departure. He is preparing them not simply to survive (they will initially be devastated and confused) but to thrive, forming a community of love that serves as a witness to the world. Now in John 14:1–31 Jesus doubles down on this loving preparation of his followers. He tells them that one day they will be with him where he is going. Until that time, he will provide all they need to abound in fruitful, joyful living. They need not be troubled. He will give them his peace.

The Big Picture

The loving Jesus reassures his disciples, granting them his peace and preparing them to thrive in his absence.

Reflection and Discussion

Read through the complete passage for this study, John 14:1–31. Then review the following questions and record your responses. (For further background, see the *ESV Study Bible*, pages 2052–2054, or visit esv.org.)

We have seen that John 13:1 frames everything Jesus does in John 13–17 as being motivated by his overwhelming love ("to the end") for his disciples. How do we see Jesus' love displayed specifically in John 14:1–31?

Identify the statement that frames this passage, appearing in verse 1 and again in verse 27. What does Jesus mean when he urges the disciples, "Let not your hearts be troubled"? What might be troubling them? How does Jesus' exhortation show his loving care for them?

Jesus provides a way for the disciples not to be troubled, and he mentions it at the beginning and end of chapter 14. In verse 1, immediately after stating, "Do not let your hearts be troubled," he goes on: "Believe in God; believe also in me." How does belief in God and Jesus push out worry and fear in the hearts of the disciples? Now look at verse 29: "I have told you before it takes place, so that when it does take place you may believe." Compare this to John 13:19. What exactly do you think Jesus is calling his disciples to believe? How will this push worry and fear from their hearts?

What reassuring evidence of Jesus' love for his disciples does he provide in verses 1–6? Jesus has already told the disciples that they cannot come where he is going (13:33), but what good news does he now share? Wonderfully, Jesus' departure is not the abandonment of the disciples but rather preparation for them to enjoy his presence (and the Father's) forever in heaven.

In 14:13–14 Jesus provides more reassurance in order to keep his disciples from being troubled when he goes away. What evidence of his continuing love for them does he provide in these verses? Notice that his promise of continuing help is both very wide ("whatever you ask . . . this I will do. . . . If you ask me anything . . . I will do it") and also very focused ("whatever you ask in my name. . . . If you ask me anything in my name"). The disciples' requests that are genuinely motivated by a desire for Jesus' glory and the advancement of his kingdom (not selfish or sinful requests) will be granted. Even in his absence Jesus will provide everything his disciples need for fruitful, joyful living.

Verses 16–17 provide additional evidence of Jesus' love, providing another reason the disciples need not be troubled by his absence. What promise does Jesus make to them here? In what way will Jesus be even closer to his disciples after his departure than before? According to verse 26, what will the Helper, the Holy Spirit, do for the disciples?

In verses 18–19 Jesus provides yet another reason for the disciples to be hopeful rather than fretful. What does he promise here? Do you understand this as a promise of his resurrection, of the coming of the Holy Spirit, or of Jesus' return at the end of the age? The reference to "seeing" Jesus and to his resurrection life perhaps favors a reference to his resurrection appearances. This helps to explain why Jesus does not simply ascend directly to the Father after his resurrection. He wants to reassure and empower his disciples.

In verses 28–29 Jesus stokes the disciples' belief in him by telling them what is going to happen before it happens. And he says that the response of the disciples to his imminent departure should be joy (14:28). What reason does he offer for this surprising claim?

Jesus wants his disciples to live transformed lives of love after his crucifixion. We see this desired outcome in verses 15, 21, 23. What do you think it means to keep Jesus' "commandments" and his "word"? Compare John 13:34–35; 15:12.

Jesus makes another solemn and stunning claim about what the disciples will do after his departure: "Whoever believes in me will also do the works that I do; and greater works than these will he do, because I am going to the Father"

(14:12). What do you think Jesus means here? How is it possible to do greater works than he did?

Read through the following three sections on *Gospel Glimpses*, *Whole-Bible Connections*, and *Theological Soundings*. Then take time to consider the *Personal Implications* these sections have for you.

Gospel Glimpses

JESUS WAS TROUBLED IN OUR PLACE. The word "troubled" in 14:1, 27 ("Let not your hearts be troubled") is the same word used in 13:21, where John says that "Jesus was troubled in his spirit." Jesus was troubled about Judas's betrayal and his own coming death. But he told his disciples *not* to be troubled. Is Jesus urging his disciples to have an experience he himself does not share? No. Rather, Jesus experiences trouble in his spirit *so that* his followers do not need to be troubled. Jesus experiences betrayal, crucifixion, and divine judgment so that his followers may avoid God's judgment and instead experience everlasting peace, being fully persuaded of God's eternal love for us. Jesus was troubled in our place.

JESUS LOVES US. Let us pause to *personalize* what we are seeing in John 14. It is true that Jesus is speaking to his original disciples in the first instance, but we know he has us in mind as well (17:20). And we remember from 20:30–31 that this Gospel is meant to be read and applied personally. So, if we are Jesus' followers, we can take a moment to apply to our own hearts the truths we are seeing in John 14. Jesus is preparing heaven for *us*. Jesus hears and answers *our* requests in his name. Jesus lives within *us* by his Holy Spirit. The resurrected Christ appeared to his first disciples, and *we* have their written accounts in the Bible. We also have the clear record that he knew in advance everything that would happen to him. Will we receive and savor Jesus' love for us? Will we seek, in response, to spread his love to other believers?

Whole-Bible Connections

I AM THE WAY, THE TRUTH, THE LIFE. In 14:4–11 Jesus says that the disciples know the way to where he is going. Through his interactions with Thomas and Philip it becomes clear that the "way" Jesus is going (i.e., his death, which will be his means of returning to God) will become the "way" for his followers to meet God. It is not just the way Jesus *takes* but the way he *becomes* for his disciples. Jesus' famous claim in 14:6, "I am the way, and the truth, and the life," brings together and fulfills many significant themes from the Old and New Testaments. Jesus provides access to the very presence of God (access that only the high priest of Israel enjoyed in the tabernacle's Most Holy Place, once a year). Jesus is the ultimate embodiment of the truth of God, greater even than the Law and Prophets. Jesus can provide spiritual life to those who believe in him (3:16) because the Father has granted him to have life within himself (5:26).

THE PARACLETE. In 14:16–17 Jesus promises to send another "Helper," the Spirit of truth. The Greek word *paraklētos* can be rendered "helper" or "advocate" (cf. additional references to the Paraclete in 14:26; 15:26; 16:7). Notice that Jesus says the Father will send *another* helper (14:16). In 1 John Jesus himself is called by this same word: "My little children, I am writing these things to you so that you may not sin. But if anyone does sin, we have an advocate [*paraklētos*] with the Father, Jesus Christ the righteous" (1 John 2:1). As the people of God, we receive the help and advocacy of God the Son and God the Holy Spirit.

Theological Soundings

BELIEF IN GOD AND JESUS. In John 14:1 Jesus says to his followers, "Believe in God; believe also in me." The statements are nearly identical, and, unless Jesus is God, it is an audacious and even blasphemous way of speaking. If any preacher stood in the pulpit and said, "Believe in God; believe also in me," he would rightly be fired immediately! Jesus' claim indicates that he agrees with Thomas's later assessment of the resurrected Jesus: "My Lord and my God!" (20:28). Further confirmation of Jesus' claim to deity in this passage is his word to Philip: "Whoever has seen me has seen the Father" (14:9).

GREATER WORKS. Jesus' solemn declaration in 14:12 ("Truly, truly, I say to you") that whoever believes in him will do the works he does and will do "greater works than these" has puzzled readers. How can Jesus' followers do greater works than Jesus? He does not mean that his disciples will heal people more effectively or be able to multiply fewer loaves and fish to feed greater crowds. It is important to note Jesus' reason for the greater works: "Because I am going to the Father." This is a reference to his atoning death on the cross and his powerful resurrection. After Jesus' death his followers will love people and offer them salvation on the basis of his completed redemptive work. That is something not even Jesus did, for the simple reason that he had not yet died. So the works of Jesus' followers will be greater because their ministry will occur at a later stage of salvation history.[1]

Personal Implications

Take time to reflect on the implications of John 14:1–31 for your own life today. Make notes below on the personal implications for your walk with the Lord of (1) the *Gospel Glimpses*, (2) the *Whole-Bible Connections*, (3) the *Theological Soundings*, and (4) this passage as a whole.

1. Gospel Glimpses

2. Whole-Bible Connections

3. Theological Soundings

4. John 14:1–31

As You Finish This Unit . . .

Take a moment now to ask for the Lord's blessing and help as you continue in this study of John 13–17. Take a moment also to look back through this unit of study, to reflect on some key things that the Lord may be teaching you, and perhaps to highlight and underline these things to review in the future.

Definitions

[1] **Salvation history** – The Bible's description of God's unfolding plan of salvation through time.

Week 6: Abiding in the Vine

John 15:1–17

The Place of the Passage

The prospect of Jesus' imminent death has overshadowed John 13–14. Judas has departed to betray Jesus. Peter's denials have been foretold. The disciples need peace for their troubled hearts. Although the loving Savior weaves throughout these chapters the prospect of heaven, the promise of the Holy Spirit, the joy of brotherly love, and the hope of doing greater works, still the scene has a cast of darkness and heaviness: "And it was night" (13:30). Into this darkness Jesus now speaks the last of his seven great "I am" statements, one of his most famous self-descriptions, an image that is at once urgently important and tremendously joy-giving.

The Big Picture

Jesus is the true vine, the source and center of all God's blessings for his people.

Reflection and Discussion

Read through the complete passage for this study, John 15:1–17. Then review the following questions and record your responses. (For further background, see the *ESV Study Bible*, pages 2054–2056, or visit esv.org.)

We have seen that John 13:1 frames everything that Jesus does in John 13–17 as being motivated by his overwhelming love ("to the end") for his disciples. How do we see Jesus' love displayed specifically in 15:1–17?

In verse 1 Jesus does not say, "I am the vine" (though he will say that in 15:5). Instead he says, "I am the true vine." Why does he say it that way? If Jesus is the true vine, who or what is not?

To abide in Jesus means to remain in Jesus. What is the opposite of abiding? Jesus is not interested in momentary belief, temporary loyalty, or fleeting excitement. Do you know people who have abided in Jesus for a long time? What are they like? How do they live?

Jesus will imminently depart from his disciples. In light of that, how do you think Jesus' command to "abide in me" might encourage them?

Jesus issues a warning in verse 2: "Every branch in me that does not bear fruit he takes away." He expands on this in verse 6, where he says that those who do not abide in him are thrown like branches into the fire and burned. What does Jesus mean? Who are the branches that do not bear fruit? Are they immature Christians, or non-Christians? It seems from verses 2, 6 that obedience to Jesus is necessary in order to escape God's final judgment. But how does this avoid becoming a religion of works?

Jesus says his disciples are already clean (15:3; cf. 13:10–11). What does he mean? How have they become clean?

What do you think Jesus means when he says that "the branch cannot bear fruit by itself" (15:4) and "apart from me you can do nothing" (15:5)? Do not even unbelievers do kind deeds and noble acts? How might Jesus' words simultaneously humble his followers and give us hope?

Jesus says, "Ask whatever you wish, and it will be done for you" (15:7). This is an amazing promise! Look closely at the first half of verse 7: How does Jesus put guardrails and guidelines around this promise? Compare this to 14:13–14; 15:16. How might these verses shape your own prayers?

Compare verse 4 ("Abide in me, and I in you") with verse 7 ("If you abide in me, and my words abide in you"). What is the connection between Jesus' abiding in us and his words' abiding in us?

Why does Jesus tell his disciples to "Abide in me" (15:4) and "Abide in my love" (15:9)? What is the connection between those two instructions? According to verse 10, what is the connection between obedience and abiding in love, both in our lives and in Jesus' life?

What does it mean for the disciples' joy to be "full" (15:11)? How might this promise particularly encourage Jesus' disciples in the face of his imminent death/departure?

Notice in verses 12–17 that Jesus returns to the theme of loving one another (cf. 13:34–35). What is the connection between abiding in Jesus (15:1–11) and loving one another (15:12–17)?

Read through the following three sections on *Gospel Glimpses*, *Whole-Bible Connections*, and *Theological Soundings*. Then take time to consider the *Personal Implications* these sections have for you.

Gospel Glimpses

BEARING FRUIT. Jesus tells his disciples, "I chose you and appointed you that you should go and bear fruit and that your fruit should abide" (15:16). This is a crucially important corrective to some forms of contemporary Christianity that focus only on getting people "saved" and into heaven. Jesus says his purpose in choosing his followers is that they bear abiding fruit, which means lasting obedience and good deeds in fulfillment of God's purposes. The purpose of a branch is to bear fruit. The purpose of Christians is to bear spiritual fruit. We are to love other believers, bear witness to God's mission to the world, obey Christ's commands, and abound in good works for God's glory. According to Jesus, God himself is committed to helping us bear more fruit, even when that involves disciplining us (15:2). Jesus' followers cannot take ultimate credit for the fruit we produce, since it all comes from Jesus as we abide in him (15:4–5).

ABIDING IN LOVE. Jesus tells his disciples to "Abide in me" (15:4) and "Abide in my love" (15:9). Jesus supplements the image of the vine by making clear that our connection with him is an abiding in his love. We remain in Jesus by allowing ourselves to bask in and receive his affection, kindness, and care for us. The reason it is a joy, not a chore, to remain in a strong, enduring marriage is that each spouse enjoys the love of the other. Neither wants to walk away from that love, so they both remain. The same is true for us and Jesus. We remain in him as we daily savor his love for us.

FRIENDS OF JESUS. Remarkably, Jesus tells his followers, "You are my friends" (15:14) and "I have called you friends" (15:15). It was extremely rare in the Old

Testament for someone to be called a friend of God. Abraham received that honor (2 Chron. 20:7; Isa. 41:8), as did Moses (Ex. 33:11). In this passage Jesus extends the privilege of friendship to all his followers. Lest we fail to accord Jesus the honor he is due, let us remember that our relationship with him is not fully reciprocal. He commands us (John 15:14, 17), he makes known to us what he has heard from the Father (15:15), and he chose us (15:16). Moreover, as our friend, Jesus manifested the greatest possible love by laying down his life for us at the cross (15:13). Yes, it is true we are his friends, but he is the infinitely greater Friend!

Whole-Bible Connections

JESUS IS THE TRUE VINE. In Isaiah 5:1–7 and Psalm 80:8–19 the metaphor of a vineyard or vine is used to describe the people of Israel. Asaph, the author of Psalm 80, says to God, "You brought a vine out of Egypt; you drove out the nations and planted it" (Ps. 80:8). But, alas, Israel repeatedly sinned, and the result was God's judgment. The vine was burned and devoured. Psalm 80 is a community lament for all that has been lost through the rebellion and failure of God's people, who were not the vine they were supposed to be. This background explains why Jesus says, "I am the true vine." Just as he is the true temple (cf. John 2:19–22), so he is the true Israel. God's people now receive spiritual life and experience the blessings of God not by being born into a particular ethnic group but by being united to Jesus Christ through faith. Jesus gathers and blesses "his own," the new community of his followers, Jew and Gentile (John 13:1).

THE FIRE OF JUDGMENT. Jesus says in verse 2, "Every branch in me that does not bear fruit he takes away." In this passage "fruit" refers to the good things, including obedience to Jesus' commands and loving one another, that God produces in believers through their union with Jesus. Notice that God takes away every branch that does not bear that good fruit. The best way to understand "takes away" is in light of verse 6, where Jesus explains, "If anyone does not abide in me he is thrown away like a branch and withers; and the branches are gathered, thrown into the fire, and burned." In the Bible fire is a common symbol of divine judgment (Isa. 30:27; Matt. 3:12). So Jesus is saying that those who fail to abide in him, and therefore do not bear the fruit of obedience, will come under God's judgment, the final and ultimate expression of which is hell.[1] Although such people may appear to be true believers, they are not. Jesus' teaching here does not promote a religion of works, in which God's favor is earned through obedience. Rather, the presence or absence of spiritual fruit demonstrates whether one is in spiritual union with Jesus.

Theological Soundings

THE PROMISE OF ANSWERED PRAYER. Jesus promises his disciples, "If you abide in me, and my words abide in you, ask whatever you wish, and it will be done for you" (15:7). Further, he says, "I chose you and appointed you that you should go and bear fruit and that your fruit should abide, so that whatever you ask the Father in my name, he may give it to you" (15:16). As we abide in Jesus, bearing abiding fruit, we come to care about what he cares about. As his words abide in us, they transform our thinking, desires, and choices. To the extent that this is the case, God will do for us whatever we desire, because our desires will be his (cf. Ps. 37:4). This is ultimate freedom: to want the things God wants. It is the experience of the citizens of heaven. God never needs to say no there. Every desire is perfected and fulfilled.

THE NEED FOR OBEDIENCE. This passage speaks frequently of "abiding" in Jesus. This may sound somewhat passive (like "Let go and let God"), even mystical. Nothing could be further from the truth, as we see from Jesus' words in John 15:10: "If you keep my commandments, you will abide in my love, just as I have kept my Father's commandments and abide in his love." Abiding in Jesus' love is not simply an ineffable feeling. It is evidenced in real, practical, nitty-gritty, daily obedience to his commandments. If he tells us to do something, we do it. He is our authority. In John's Gospel the focus of Jesus' commandments is love for his followers (e.g. 15:12–13). We abide in Jesus as we trust him and obey his commands. We take no credit for our obedience, because we know we can do nothing apart from Jesus (15:5).

Personal Implications

Take time to reflect on the implications of John 15:1–17 for your own life today. Make notes below on the personal implications for your walk with the Lord of (1) the *Gospel Glimpses*, (2) the *Whole-Bible Connections*, (3) the *Theological Soundings*, and (4) this passage as a whole.

1. Gospel Glimpses

2. Whole-Bible Connections

3. Theological Soundings

4. John 15:1–17

As You Finish This Unit . . .

Take a moment now to ask for the Lord's blessing and help as you continue in this study of John 13–17. Take a moment also to look back through this unit of study, to reflect on some key things that the Lord may be teaching you, and perhaps to highlight and underline these things to review in the future.

Definitions

[1] **Hell** – In the teaching of Jesus a real place of "unquenchable fire" (Mark 9:43). It is a place of eternal torment under God's wrath for those who have not repented and placed their trust in Jesus Christ.

Week 7: Hated by the World, Part 1

John 15:18–27

The Place of the Passage

To this point in his Farewell Discourse the main challenge Jesus has addressed has been his imminent death/departure. Compelled by overwhelming love for his disciples, he has prepared them by reassuring them of the coming of the Holy Spirit and of an eternal future together and by laying the groundwork for a remarkable community of mutual love that will continue after he is gone (13:34–35; 15:12–17). But Jesus has not yet addressed the fact that he is leaving his disciples in the middle of a hostile world. Their task is not merely to love one another but to live on mission to the very world that despises them (20:21). How will they do this? Because Jesus loves his followers to the uttermost, he now prepares them for this challenge.

The Big Picture

The world[1] has hated Jesus, and so it will hate Jesus' followers. But the triune God will empower them for effective witness to this hostile world.

Reflection and Discussion

Read through the complete passage for this study, John 15:18–27. Then review the following questions and record your responses. (For further background, see the *ESV Study Bible*, page 2056, or visit esv.org.)

We have seen that John 13:1 frames everything that Jesus does in John 13–17 as being motivated by his overwhelming love ("to the end") for his disciples. How do we see Jesus' love displayed specifically in John 15:18–27?

Jesus refers to the "world" in verse 18. Of what or whom is he speaking? Strikingly, the context of this passage indicates that the "world," a term that in John's Gospel often refers to those hostile to God, includes the Jewish religious leaders of Jesus' day, who will persecute his followers (15:25; 16:2). Hatred of Christ's followers will come both from irreligious and religious people. This still happens today. Can you think of examples?

Do you think the "if" in verse 18 implies a possibility that the world will not hate Christ's followers if Christians are kind, polite, successful, well-presented, and community-minded? Jesus in fact assumes that the world will hate his followers. We could paraphrase verse 18 like this: "If the world hates you (and that it will), then know that it has hated me before it hated you." It is crystal clear throughout Jesus' Farewell Discourse that the world has (17:14), does (15:19), and will (15:21; 16:2) hate Jesus' followers. This is why John will say in one of his letters, "Do not be surprised, brothers, that the world hates you" (1 John 3:13). How do you feel when you receive hostility from the world? Does it catch you off guard? Do you expect it?

Jesus himself will explain in 16:1, 4 why he speaks the words of 15:18–27 to his disciples: so that they can reflect later on his words (16:4) and thus be kept "from falling away" (16:1). Jesus knows there will be intense pressure on his disciples to apostatize—to abandon the faith. How might the truth of 15:18 strengthen the disciples to continue even in the face of the world's hatred? How might it reassure them? How does it reassure you?

Compare 15:12 and 15:18. Jesus goes first in loving others, and he goes first in being hated by others. What do we learn about Jesus from this? How can it encourage us in the face of opposition?

What reason for the world's hatred does Jesus highlight in verse 19–20? Jesus is not saying that the world will hate Christians only when they are silly, stupid, or insensitive. He is saying that the world will hate Christians not just at their worst but at their best—that is, the world will hate Christians as Christians.

This is a sobering truth. But Jesus' explanation of the world's hatred is also strengthening. How might it keep the disciples from falling away?

Why does Jesus' choice of his disciples provoke the world's hatred (15:19)?

In verse 21 Jesus provides another reason why the world will hate and persecute his disciples. What is the reason? How might it strengthen them against falling away?

Jesus remarks that the world does "not know him who sent me" (15:21). He is referring to the Father (cf. 3:34; 4:34; 5:23–24, 30). If Jesus includes the Jews as part of the "world," how can Jesus say that the Jews do not know God? As you consider your answer, it may be helpful to review other passages in John's Gospel prior to the Farewell Discourse (e.g., 8:39–47).

How has the ministry of Jesus increased the guilt of those who oppose him (15:22–24)?

How might Jesus' words in verses 26–27 strengthen and encourage his disciples? According to verse 26, who will empower them for effective witness?

Read through the following three sections on *Gospel Glimpses*, *Whole-Bible Connections*, and *Theological Soundings*. Then take time to consider the *Personal Implications* these sections have for you.

Gospel Glimpses

CONNECTED TO THE VINE. This passage is full of very bad news, particularly in its focus on the certain and constant hatred of the world for believers. But woven throughout is the beautiful, hope-giving theme of union with Christ. As believers obey Jesus' call to "abide in me" (15:4), they will be vitally, permanently connected to him in the closest possible union. Although this will lead to hatred and persecution from the world, the world's reactions will confirm that the union is real. The world's persecution of Jesus will be matched by its persecution of those who are united to Jesus (15:18, 20). Jesus reminds his disciples of this union, telling them that "you have been with me from the beginning" (15:27) and that the persecution they endure will be "on account of my name" (15:21). This ennobles their suffering, giving it great purpose. Persecuted believers can remind themselves of the sweet truth that they are branches united to the vine.

THE COMING OF THE HELPER. Jesus promises to send the Helper from the Father to his disciples: the "Spirit of truth, who proceeds from the Father" (15:26).

Notice that the Spirit comes from both Jesus and the Father. Jesus' promise will be fulfilled at Pentecost (Acts 2). The coming of the Spirit ensures that the disciples will indeed bear witness even to a hostile world (John 15:27). When they testify to Christ, the Spirit will be working in and through what they say.

Whole-Bible Connections

HATED FOR BEING CHOSEN. In verse 19 Jesus identifies his choice of the disciples as the reason that the world hates them. This is because Jesus' choice means his followers now belong to him and submit to him. That places Christians radically out of step with the world, which does not love or obey Christ. This is a fundamental clash, even if we are the kindest, gentlest, and most loving of Christians. We were chosen by Christ (every Christian has been), and we do not belong to the world (no Christian does). Jesus says we are hated by the world not because we are *bad* Christians but because we *are* Christians. Genesis 4:1–16 and Hebrews 11:4 highlight the age-old enmity that the world manifests toward those who follow God. It is an ancient reality, not a new one. Christians should not be surprised when they are on the receiving end of the world's hatred (1 John 3:12).

HATRED IN FULFILLMENT OF SCRIPTURE. By speaking of "their Law" (John 15:25) Jesus makes clear that "the world" he references in this passage includes those among the Jews who reject him. He says that the Jews' hatred fulfills Psalm 69:4, a psalm in which David describes the suffering he experiences from God's enemies. They persecute him not because he has done wrong but because he has been faithful to God. David bears reproach "for [his] sake" (Ps. 69:7) and cries out to God for salvation. Jesus appeals to this psalm because he perceives the similarity between his situation and David's. They are both hated without cause. So the hatred directed toward Jesus and his followers fulfills Scripture. This is surely hope-giving for Jesus' disciples, because it means that the world's hatred, as a fulfillment of Scripture, is under the sovereign hand of God. Moreover, others before them (none less than King David, and Jesus himself) have also been persecuted without cause. They are not alone.

Theological Soundings

GUILTY OF SIN. The Bible teaches that every human being is sinful and has fallen short of the glory of God (Rom. 3:23). So, when Jesus says that, if he had not spoken and done works among his enemies, they "would not have been guilty of sin" (John 15:22, cf. 15:24), he is not speaking of all sin, claiming that apart from his ministry they would have been considered sinlessly perfect. Rather, he is referring specifically to the sin of rejecting God's revelation through

Jesus. His enemies' hatred and rejection demonstrate that they do not actually know God (though they would surely claim to know him) and are in fact opposed to the ways of God.

EMPOWERED BY THE TRIUNE GOD. The early church did not articulate a full-orbed, carefully defined doctrine of the Trinity until after the time of John's Gospel. But in verse 26 we can see some of the crucial elements. And, significantly, Jesus is not formulating abstract doctrine. Rather, he is interested in describing how God will empower the disciples for the sake of witness to a hostile world. The Spirit (called the "Helper" and the "Spirit of truth") proceeds from the Father, the Son sends the Spirit, and the Spirit bears witness to the Son. Father, Son, and Holy Spirit are all active! Christians may be tempted to hate the world that hates them. But we know *God* does not hate it: "God [in this way] loved the world, that he gave his only Son" (3:16). Christians may be tempted to shelter far away from the world that hates them, erecting high walls and having as little as possible to do with it. But this is not what the triune God intends. He gives us everything we need in order to bear witness (15:27).

Personal Implications

Take time to reflect on the implications of John 15:18–27 for your own life today. Make notes below on the personal implications for your walk with the Lord of (1) the *Gospel Glimpses*, (2) the *Whole-Bible Connections*, (3) the *Theological Soundings*, and (4) this passage as a whole.

1. Gospel Glimpses

2. Whole-Bible Connections

3. Theological Soundings

4. John 15:18–27

As You Finish This Unit . . .

Take a moment now to ask for the Lord's blessing and help as you continue in this study of John 13–17. Take a moment also to look back through this unit of study, to reflect on some key things that the Lord may be teaching you, and perhaps to highlight and underline these things to review in the future.

Definitions

[1] **World** – Those who do not know Christ; humanity in rebellion against God.

Week 8: Hated by the World, Part 2

John 16:1–15

The Place of the Passage

Good parents know that when they need to inform their children of some difficult news (a grandparent has fallen ill, a pet has died, an accident has occurred), the most loving thing to do is to express support and compassion, then share the news clearly. Although speaking may provoke tears and pain, the alternatives (keeping silent or distorting the truth) are unloving. We have seen how Jesus, at the beginning of his Farewell Discourse, expresses his overwhelming love for his disciples by washing their feet, a symbol of his sin-cleansing death. Having assured them of his care, he then shares hard news with them, taking it one step at a time. First, he focuses on his impending absence, encouraging them with promises of provision while he is gone. Next, he warns them about the hostility of the world, which will be expressed through hatred and persecution. In our passage he is even more specific about what the world will do.

The Big Picture

Spurred on by love for his disciples, Jesus increases the specificity of his warning to them while also increasing the specificity of his promise regarding the help they will receive from the triune God to empower their gospel witness.

Reflection and Discussion

Read through the complete passage for this study, John 16:1–15. Then review the following questions and record your responses. (For further background, see the *ESV Study Bible*, pages 2056–2057, or visit esv.org.)

We have seen that John 13:1 frames everything that Jesus does in John 13–17 as being motivated by his overwhelming love ("to the end") for his disciples. How do we see Jesus' love displayed specifically in John 16:1–15?

We noticed in Week 7 that Jesus warns his disciples of coming opposition in order to prevent them from falling away when such opposition occurs (16:1). Can you think of situations in which you were alerted to impending difficulty or danger? How did the advance notice help you prepare and endure? Did you receive it as an expression of love?

Why will some who kill Christians believe they are offering service to God (16:2)? Can you think of specific examples? See Acts 8:3; 9:1–2; 22:3–5; 26:4–11; Galatians 1:13–14. Did Saul/Paul understand his persecution of Christians to be God-honoring or God-dishonoring? Was he ashamed or proud of this later? Why?

According to Jesus in John 16:3, what is the reality concerning those who believe they know and serve God?

When God's people are persecuted, they may be tempted to believe that God has abandoned them or is angry with them. How might verse 4 undermine that wrong belief?

According to the second half of verse 4, why has Jesus not previously revealed the full extent of the disciples' future suffering? According to the first half of verse 5, why is he sharing it with them now? Why did Jesus' presence with the disciples mean he did not need to reveal everything?

Why does Jesus say in verse 5 that no one is asking him where he is going? Did Peter not ask him that question in 13:36? Note the present tense of the verb "asks" in 16:5. Does this help in understanding what Jesus means? Some time has elapsed, and some distance has been traveled (cf. 14:31) since Peter's question.

How does Jesus in 16:7 address the disciples' sorrow? Why do you think Jesus begins with the words "I tell you the truth"? Is not everything that Jesus says true? Why is it advantageous for the disciples if Jesus goes away?

Notice how the truth packed into 15:26–27 is now beautifully unfolded and expanded in 16:7–15. In both passages Jesus promises the coming of the Spirit of truth. But what additional information does he now provide?

What will the Helper do for the world when Jesus sends him (16:8–11)? How will this aspect of the Spirit's work undergird and empower the disciples' witness?

Why is the Helper called the "Spirit of truth" in verse 13? How will he guide the disciples into "all the truth" in the days to come? How will this empower their gospel witness to a hostile world?

Read through the following three sections on *Gospel Glimpses*, *Whole-Bible Connections*, and *Theological Soundings*. Then take time to consider the *Personal Implications* these sections have for you.

Gospel Glimpses

HE WILL CONVICT THE WORLD. Sweet gospel hope is found in Jesus' promise that the Helper (i.e., the Holy Spirit) will "convict the world" (16:8). Recall that in John's Gospel "the world" refers typically not to the planet, the universe, or all humanity but to those people who are opposed to God. Jesus' words demonstrate that being part of the world does not necessarily mean that someone will *always* be so. The Spirit brings conviction. There is hope for rebels.

THE RULER OF THIS WORLD IS JUDGED. Jesus' description of how it is that the Helper will convict the world is simultaneously sobering and superb news. In verse 11 Jesus calls Satan the "ruler of this world" (cf. 12:31; 14:30). By referring to him in this way, Jesus recognizes Satan's vast spiritual influence over those who live in opposition to God (cf. Jesus' words in 8:39–47 to the Jews who oppose him). John himself will say in one of his letters, "The whole world lies in the power of the evil one" (1 John 5:19). Satan is a mighty foe. But, while all of this is sobering, it is not the end of the story. Satan has no authority over Jesus himself. Jesus dies not because Satan conquers or outmaneuvers him but because Jesus lovingly obeys the Father (John 14:30–31). And in 16:11 Jesus goes on to say that "the ruler of this world *is judged*." This is superb news. Jesus' death on the cross brings about Satan's downfall, as Jesus has already explained: "Now is the judgment of this world; now will the ruler of this world be cast out" (12:31). The cross ensures Satan's doom.

Whole-Bible Connections

THE COMING OF THE SPIRIT. The Old Testament prophets anticipated the coming of God's kingdom as a time when God would pour out his Spirit upon his people. "I will pour water on the thirsty land, and streams on the dry ground; I will pour my Spirit upon your offspring, and my blessing on your descendants" (Isa. 44:3). "I will give you a new heart, and a new spirit I will put within you. And I will remove the heart of stone from your flesh and give you a heart of flesh. And I will put my Spirit within you, and cause you to walk in my statutes and be careful to obey my rules" (Ezek. 36:26–27). Against the backdrop of this fervent expectation (see also Joel 2:28–32 and many other Old Testament passages) the coming of the Helper can be seen as the enormously important event it actually is. God inaugurates his kingdom as the Helper comes to Jesus' followers.

Theological Soundings

THE SPIRIT GUIDES THE DISCIPLES. Not only does the Helper convict the world (John 16:8–11), but he also guides Jesus' disciples into "all the truth" (16:12–15). This promise finds initial and particular fulfillment in and through the original disciples, particularly as they write or direct the writing of the New Testament books (cf. 14:26). But, as with the rest of John 13–17, Jesus' words have a further, secondary fulfillment for future followers, including us. The Holy Spirit guides us into truth, helping us more fully to understand Jesus, who is the truth (14:6). The Holy Spirit ensures that believers are confident in the truth and that those he is drawing from the world are prepared for gospel witness. Again, we see here that the triune God gives Jesus' followers everything necessary for effective witness to a hostile world.

THE DEITY OF THE SPIRIT. Jesus says the Holy Spirit will "declare to you the things that are to come" (16:13). In Isaiah, only God is able to know and declare what is to come: "Behold, the former things have come to pass, and new things I now declare; before they spring forth I tell you of them" (Isa. 42:9). "Who is like me? Let him proclaim it. Let him declare and set it before me, since I appointed an ancient people. Let them declare what is to come, and what will happen" (Isa. 44:7; cf. Isa. 46:9–10; *ESV Study Bible*, page 1326). This Old Testament backdrop demonstrates that the Holy Spirit is fully God (see also 1 Cor. 2:11). As God, he knows and declares the future.

Personal Implications

Take time to reflect on the implications of John 16:1–15 for your own life today. Make notes below on the personal implications for your walk with the Lord of (1) the *Gospel Glimpses*, (2) the *Whole-Bible Connections*, (3) the *Theological Soundings*, and (4) this passage as a whole.

1. Gospel Glimpses

2. Whole-Bible Connections

3. Theological Soundings

4. John 16:1–15

As You Finish This Unit . . .

Take a moment now to ask for the Lord's blessing and help as you continue in this study of John 13–17. Take a moment also to look back through this unit of study, to reflect on some key things that the Lord may be teaching you, and perhaps to highlight and underline these things to review in the future.

Week 9: A Call to Courage

John 16:16–33

The Place of the Passage

These verses bring us to the end of Jesus' Farewell Discourse (but not to the end of this study). Having preached one of the best sermons ever delivered (John 13–16), Jesus will immediately pray one of the best prayers ever uttered (John 17). To this point in the Farewell Discourse Jesus has prepared his disciples for his imminent departure, for their future life together, and for their task of witnessing to a hostile world. In this concluding section we see Jesus' honest and earnest assurance ("Truly, truly, I say to you" in 16:20, 23) that, while his departure will be difficult for the disciples, their sorrow will turn to joy and their confusion to clarity. Jesus' overcoming of the world secures and guarantees peace for his followers, despite the certainty of coming tribulation. For this reason they can truly "take heart" and live with courageous faith.

The Big Picture

Jesus is realistic and optimistic. He prepares his disciples for the future by telling them how bad—and how good—things will be. Importantly, the highs will be higher than the lows are low. This is why the conclusion of this passage—and of the Farewell Discourse as a whole—is Jesus' call to "take heart" on the basis of his world-overcoming death and resurrection (16:33).

Reflection and Discussion

Read through the complete passage for this study, John 16:16–33. Then review the following questions and record your responses. (For further background, see the *ESV Study Bible*, pages 2057–2058, or visit esv.org.)

We have seen that John 13:1 frames everything that Jesus does in John 13–17 as being motivated by his overwhelming love ("to the end") for his disciples. How do we see Jesus' love displayed in John 16:16–33?

John emphasizes Jesus' words in verse 16 by describing the disciples' confusion over them (16:17–18), followed by Jesus' repetition, explanation, and expansion of them (16:19–24). They must be very important words to receive such attention! What do you think Jesus means when he says, "A little while, and you will see me no longer; and again a little while, and you will see me" (16:16)?

Why does Jesus want his disciples to know that they will not see him in the immediate period after his crucifixion but will see him after he is raised from the dead? Do the disciples understand what Jesus is saying? How might his words strengthen them later (cf. 13:19; 16:4)?

Jesus emphasizes that the disciples' future joy will be greater than their present and imminent sorrow. How does the illustration of a woman's giving birth make this point (16:21)? According to verse 22, why will the disciples' sorrow turn to joy? According to verses 20, 22, is their sorrow permanent or temporary? Is their joy permanent or temporary?

With another "Truly, truly, I say to you" formula (16:23) Jesus emphatically assures his disciples of the Father's provision and invites them to ask the Father in his name for whatever they desire (16:23–24). What is Jesus' purpose in encouraging them to ask the Father (see 16:24; and see also 16:22 for the promise of future joy)? What does it mean for Jesus' followers to ask the Father "in my name" (16:23–24)?

The theme of asking the Father in Jesus' name continues in verses 26–28. This time Jesus emphasizes the eager love of the Father for the disciples (16:26–27).

According to verse 27, why does the Father love the disciples? How does Jesus expand on the truth of verse 27 through his words in verse 28?

Compare 16:28 with 13:3. The truth of Jesus' origin and destination conveyed in these two verses brackets the entire Farewell Discourse. What is the significance of these bookends? How do they shape our understanding of that which comes in between?

Jesus has contrasted the disciples' short-term sorrow with their long-term joy. In verse 25 he contrasts their present confusion with their future clarity of understanding. After his resurrection he will "tell you plainly about the Father." How does this shed light on Jesus' claim in verse 23 that "in that day" (i.e., after his resurrection) the disciples "will ask nothing of me"? How do the disciples respond in verses 29–30 to Jesus' promise of clearer speech?

Jesus offers the disciples a dose of realism in verses 31–32 as he predicts their imminent scattering and abandonment of him. In the face of this abandonment what is Jesus' strong hope?

The disciples will forsake Jesus. He knows this yet loves them unfailingly. According to verse 33, why has Jesus told his disciples these things? Despite future tribulation what is the basis for the courage ("take heart") he calls them to have? Since Jesus has not yet died and been raised how can he claim to have "overcome the world"?

Read through the following three sections on *Gospel Glimpses*, *Whole-Bible Connections*, and *Theological Soundings*. Then take time to consider the *Personal Implications* these sections have for you.

Gospel Glimpses

UNENDING JOY. One of the great themes of this section (and of the Farewell Discourse as a whole) is Jesus' promise of joy. It is particularly striking to see this in the context of a passage that assures the disciples of weeping, lament, sorrow, and tribulation. The joy that Jesus promises must be surpassingly great to eclipse the hardship coming their way. Jesus uses the image of a woman whose joy at the birth of her baby causes her no longer to remember the anguish of childbirth (16:21). As some commentators have noted, the Old Testament prophets employed the metaphor of childbirth to describe the future suffering and pain of God's people—suffering that would be followed by the relief of messianic salvation (e.g., Isa. 21:2–3; 26:16–21; 66:7–14). As we studied in Week 6, the prophets saw the last days as a time of exuberant joy. And that time has now come. Jesus highlights the unending, climactic joy his disciples will experience.

I HAVE OVERCOME THE WORLD. The basis for Jesus' assurance of peace (cf. 14:27) and his call to courage in verse 33 is his overcoming of the world, a reference to his imminent death and resurrection. Although Jesus has not yet been crucified and raised, these events are so certain that he can speak of his victory as already having happened. Jesus' victory over his enemies ("the world") guarantees the victory of his followers (cf. 1 John 2:13–14; 4:4; 5:4–5). This is good news! Christians are not called to be naively cheerful or optimistic. Our peace and courage are rooted in the saving work of Christ himself.

Whole-Bible Connections

PLAIN SPEECH. In the Gospels Jesus often speaks in parables and sometimes uses obscure language. Contrary to popular opinion, parables are not sermon illustrations meant to clarify otherwise difficult teaching. Rather, the parables themselves can be hard to grasp. For this reason they function as a sort of litmus test: Are those who hear the parables sufficiently engaged spiritually to press into their meaning and perceive the mystery of the kingdom? In this respect Jesus' parables are akin to his favorite self-designation as the "Son of Man." Those without spiritual perception will hear "Son of Man" to mean nothing more than "human being," as the term is used by the prophet Ezekiel (e.g., Ezek. 3:3–4, 10, 17). But those in whom God is working may hear overtones of the divine Son of Man in Daniel 7:13–14 and wonder whether Jesus is in fact making a staggeringly great claim for himself. In John's Gospel Jesus often speaks in ways that are not understood (e.g., John 3:3–4; 6:52–66; 7:32–36) or are understood only later (e.g., 2:18–22; 12:16; 13:7). In 16:25 Jesus acknowledges that he has spoken to the disciples in "figures of speech," and he promises that at the time of his resurrection he will "tell you plainly about the Father" (see Luke 24:27; Acts 1:3).

THE SCATTERING OF THE DISCIPLES. In John 16:32 Jesus tells the disciples that an hour is coming, and has come, "when you will be scattered, each to his own home, and will leave me alone." Jesus is likely alluding here to Zechariah 13:7: "Strike the shepherd, and the sheep will be scattered," which is quoted in Matthew 26:31. As we have seen already in the Farewell Discourse, the events surrounding Jesus' death are fulfillments of the Scriptures (cf. John 13:18) and thus within the sovereign plan of God.

Theological Soundings

PRAYING IN JESUS' NAME. Jesus assures his followers that whatever they ask of the Father "in my name" will be given to them (16:23; cf. 14:13), and he says that in the time of his resurrection his disciples will "ask in my name" (16:26). As discussed in the *ESV Study Bible* (page 2053), praying in Jesus' name means praying "in a way consistent with his character and will" (since in the ancient world a person's name represented his character) and also "coming to God in the authority of Jesus." These passages do not require every faithful prayer of believers to end with the phrase "in Jesus' name." However, if those words remind us to pray in line with Jesus' will and to come to the Father through Jesus, they can be very helpful.

JESUS' ADVENT AND DEPARTURE. It is illuminating to compare 13:3 with 16:28. "Jesus, knowing that the Father had given all things into his hands, and that he had come from God and was going back to God" (13:3); "I came from the Father and have come into the world, and now I am leaving the world and going to the Father" (16:28). These verses form the two great bookends of the Farewell Discourse. Together they demonstrate the dual realities that Jesus' life did not begin with his birth nor end with his death and resurrection. Everything Jesus says and does in the Farewell Discourse (and in the rest of his earthly life) is endued with the authority of the one who enjoys eternal glory with the Father.

Personal Implications

Take time to reflect on the implications of John 16:16–33 for your own life today. Make notes below on the personal implications for your walk with the Lord of (1) the *Gospel Glimpses*, (2) the *Whole-Bible Connections*, (3) the *Theological Soundings*, and (4) this passage as a whole.

1. Gospel Glimpses

2. Whole-Bible Connections

3. Theological Soundings

4. John 16:16–33

As You Finish This Unit . . .

Take a moment now to ask for the Lord's blessing and help as you continue in this study of John 13–17. Take a moment also to look back through this unit of study, to reflect on some key things that the Lord may be teaching you, and perhaps to highlight and underline these things to review in the future.

Week 10: The Prayer of Jesus, Part 1

John 17:1–26

The Place of the Passage

In John 17 Jesus moves from preaching to prayer—from speaking with his disciples to speaking with his Father. So, as we approach this chapter of Scripture, let us ponder its awesome mystery. The Gospel of John is clear that Jesus is God (cf. the bookends of John 1:1 and 20:28). That means that in John 17, which is by far the longest prayer of Jesus recorded in the Gospels, we overhear God speaking with *God*. This is intratrinitarian fellowship and conversation! Here we glimpse the communion of God the Son with God the Father. Let us approach this chapter with reverence and awe. And let us catch our breath as well, enjoying this moment of divine conversation, because as soon as it ends the readers of John's Gospel will be thrown headlong into the fast-moving events of Jesus' arrest, trial, and crucifixion.

The Big Picture

We will devote two sessions to our study of this remarkable prayer. In this first week we will examine the overall flow of the prayer and then focus on its first section (17:1–5). In doing so we will discover that, while this prayer is for the twelve disciples, it is also far bigger than that.

Reflection and Discussion

Read through the complete passage for this study, John 17:1–26. Then review the following questions and record your responses. (For further background, see the *ESV Study Bible*, pages 2058–2060, or visit esv.org.)

We have seen that John 13:1 frames everything that Jesus does in John 13–17 as being motivated by his overwhelming love ("to the end") for his disciples. How do we see Jesus' love displayed specifically in John 17:1–26, particularly in verses 1–5?

One way to see the overall flow of this prayer is to observe whom Jesus is praying for and what Jesus is asking the Father to do. Scan down through verses 1–26. What do you notice about the whom and the what of Jesus' prayer?

For whom is Jesus mainly praying in verses 1–5, and what is he asking (see 17:1, 5)? For which group does Jesus begin to pray in verse 6? Who are the "people whom you gave me out of the world" (17:6)? Notice that Jesus says in verse 9, "I am praying for them." What does Jesus ask for them? In addition to his first disciples, for whom does Jesus begin to pray in verse 20? What are his requests for this additional group?

A Prayer beyond the Disciples (17:1–5)

Why is it significant that Jesus begins his prayer in verses 1–5 by referencing his relationship with the Father rather than by making requests for his disciples (he will get to those in 17:6–26)? It is important for us to see that this prayer is bigger than the disciples—it is about the eternal life of the triune God!

In verse 1 how does John describe Jesus' physical posture? Why is this description significant? Since God is everywhere, not just in heaven, why do you think Jesus lifts his eyes to heaven? Recall the Lord's Prayer, wherein Jesus teaches his disciples to pray, "Our Father in heaven" (Matt. 6:9). What accounts for Jesus' focus on the Father in heaven in both instances?

What does Jesus mean in John 17:1 when he says, "The hour has come"? Take a quick look at John 2:4; 7:6–8, 30; 8:20. In light of those repeated claims why is 17:1 so significant? Look also at John 12:23.

The "hour" to which Jesus refers is the hour of his death. But, given that crucifixion was a hideous, painful, shameful means of execution, how can Jesus be asking the Father to "glorify" him in this hour? Consider John 13:31–32 as you make your answer.

For what purpose does Jesus ask the Father to glorify him (17:1)? How exactly will Jesus glorify the Father? Look to verses 2–3 as you consider this.

According to verse 4, how has Jesus already glorified the Father?

In verse 5 Jesus again asks the Father to glorify him, and he now specifies the glory with which he is asking the Father to glorify him. How does Jesus describe that glory (see the second half of 17:5)? This is astounding! How do Jesus' words to the Father in verse 5 help you to appreciate even more fully the awesome privilege of overhearing this prayer?

Read through the following three sections on *Gospel Glimpses*, *Whole-Bible Connections*, and *Theological Soundings*. Then take time to consider the *Personal Implications* these sections have for you.

Gospel Glimpses

HOW THE SON GLORIFIES THE FATHER. The flow of thought in verses 1–3 is significant and illuminating. Jesus asks the Father to glorify him (through his death on the cross) in order that he might glorify the Father (17:1). He then specifies *how* he will glorify the Father by highlighting the Father's gift to him of authority over all flesh, to "give eternal life to all whom you have given him" (17:2). Jesus explains that eternal life consists of knowing "you, the only true God, and Jesus Christ whom you have sent" (17:3). In this context, with Jesus' reference in verse 1 to his imminent crucifixion, it seems clear that Jesus' death is what allows him to grant eternal life—intimate, relational knowledge of the Father and Son—to the people of God. The death of Jesus secures a people who know and love God. Their glad allegiance to God honors him. This is how the Son glorifies the Father through his death.

THE GOOD NEWS THAT GOD IS BIGGER THAN WE ARE. It is good, necessary, and joy-producing to be reminded that God is infinitely bigger than we are. That is what verses 1–5 show us. Jesus' prayer is a prayer *beyond* the disciples. He does not need the disciples in order to be glorious—he had glory from the Father before the world existed (17:5). He does not need the disciples in order to experience love—he had that with the Father before the foundation of the world (cf. 17:24). We live in a God-centered universe, and the Bible tells a God-centered story in which God is the origin, center, and goal of all things. This is very good news. But this grand biblical narrative clashes with our selfish instincts and our sinful culture, which tells a profoundly man-centered story. Ironically, when we try to place ourselves at the center of the story, things fall apart. Weak and sinful human beings cannot bear the weight of playing the lead role. It is not ours to fill. However, when we find our place in God's universe, with *God* in the leading role, our story fits where it belongs, and we thrive.

Whole-Bible Connections

IS GOD KNOWABLE? Although God is under no obligation to reveal himself to his human creation, the Bible contains key moments that show his doing exactly that. For instance in Exodus 33:19, after Moses's request to see God's glory, God replies, "I will make all my goodness pass before you and will proclaim before you my name 'The LORD.' And I will be gracious to whom I will be gracious, and will show mercy on whom I will show mercy." However, God immediately tells Moses that he cannot see God's face (his full glory—remember, God has no physical body) but rather will see his back (a smaller display of his glory; Ex. 33:20–23). The teaching of the Bible is that fallen, finite humanity can know God *truly* but not *fully*. In Jesus' prayer in John 17, therefore, we should anticipate learning more about our glorious triune God as we overhear God speaking with God. Yet we should also expect that we will not understand completely, because God is holy, while we are sinful; he is infinite, while we are finite.

Theological Soundings

OUR FATHER IN HEAVEN. As he begins his prayer, Jesus lifts his eyes to heaven. This is not because he believes God exists only in one place. Jesus knows God is omnipresent[1] (cf. Ps. 139:7–10). The great Reformer John Calvin rightly suggested that Jesus' heavenward gaze reminds us of how the majesty of God is exalted far above all creatures. Through Jesus' posture he reverently underscores God's greatness and power.

FROM TEACHING TO PRAYER. John Calvin saw Jesus' movement from teaching (John 13–16) to prayer (John 17) as an example for all Christian teachers. We will do well to heed this wise counsel. Whenever God provides a ministry opportunity, such as a conversation with our child or neighbor, leading a small group Bible study, teaching a kids' Bible class, or sharing the gospel with a coworker, we ought to mingle prayers to God with our words to people, asking God to make our ministry effective (cf. Ps. 127:1–2). As we do so, we are following the example of our Lord himself.

Personal Implications

Take time to reflect on the implications of John 17:1–26 for your own life today. Make notes below on the personal implications for your walk with the Lord of (1) the *Gospel Glimpses*, (2) the *Whole-Bible Connections*, (3) the *Theological Soundings*, and (4) this passage as a whole.

1. Gospel Glimpses

2. Whole-Bible Connections

3. Theological Soundings

4. John 17:1–26

As You Finish This Unit . . .

Take a moment now to ask for the Lord's blessing and help as you continue in this study of John 13–17. Take a moment also to look back through this unit of study, to reflect on some key things that the Lord may be teaching you, and perhaps to highlight and underline these things to review in the future.

Definitions

[1] **Omnipresent** – The biblical truth that God, who is a spirit, is present in all places and at all times.

Week 11: The Prayer of Jesus, Part 2

John 17:1–26

The Place of the Passage

In our first session on John 17 we saw that Jesus' prayer to the Father is a conversation within the eternal, triune Godhead. It is therefore far greater than, and way beyond, Jesus' disciples. But that is not the end of the story. In this second session devoted to Jesus' prayer we will see that, remarkably, the triune God concerns himself with the affairs of human beings. When God the Son, staring his imminent death full in the face, speaks to God the Father, it turns out that most of the discussion concerns Jesus' first disciples (17:6–19) and also *us*, his followers in future generations (17:20–26).

The Big Picture

On the night before his crucifixion Jesus manifests his remarkable love for his present and future followers by praying for them.

Reflection and Discussion

Read through the complete passage for this study, John 17:1–26. Then review the following questions and record your responses. (For further background, see the *ESV Study Bible*, pages 2058–2060, or visit esv.org.)

We have seen that John 13:1 frames everything that Jesus that does in John 13–17 as being motivated by his overwhelming love ("to the end") for his disciples. How do we see Jesus' love displayed in John 17:1–26, particularly in verses 6–26?

A Prayer for the First Disciples (17:6–19)

It is worth pausing to consider the implications of one very basic fact about John 17: It was overheard by someone (presumably John) and written down. Why do you think Jesus chose to pray to the Father in a manner that could be overheard? What does he intend for the disciples to learn as they listen in on his conversation with the Father? What can we learn about prayer through Jesus' desire to commune with the Father *and* to encourage people?

According to verse 9, why is Jesus praying not for the world but for the disciples? What additional reason does Jesus offer in verse 11 to explain why he is praying on behalf of the disciples? Recall that the "world" in John's Gospel typically refers to those opposed to God's people (cf. 17:14).

Review verses 6–19. What requests does Jesus make to the Father for his disciples? (Hint: See 17:11, 15, 17.)

What does it mean for the Holy Father to "keep" the disciples in his name (17:11)? According to the second half of verse 11, what is the goal of God's work of spiritual preservation?

What do you think it means for Jesus' followers to be one even as the Father and Son are one (17:11)? Is Jesus praying for *spiritual* unity? *Institutional* unity? Some of both, or something else? How is this prayer being fulfilled today? What forces or factors are working against its fulfillment?

The word "keep" used in verse 11 is used again in verse 15, where Jesus prays, "I do not ask that you take them out of the world, but that you keep them from the evil one." Who is the "evil one"? What does Jesus mean by asking God to keep the disciples from him? Do you pray similar prayers for yourself and other believers?

As we saw in our study of John 13–16, Jesus' vision for his disciples is not that they survive in a defensive crouch against a hostile world. He wants them to live on mission, taking new ground. Read verses 17–19. What will be required in order for the disciples to live on mission? Notice what Jesus says on either side of his words about mission in verse 18: God's Word (17:17) and Christ's cross ("I consecrate myself," 17:19) are vital for effective mission.

A Prayer for Us (17:20–26)

In verses 21–23 what does Jesus pray for present and future believers? According to the first part of verse 21, on what greater reality is the unity of believers modeled? According to the second part of verse 21 and verse 23, what will be the result of the unity of believers? According to verse 22, what has Christ provided in order to secure the unity of believers?

Staggeringly, in verse 22 Jesus says that the glory the Father has given him he has given to us, that we may be one even as he and the Father are one! What do you think Jesus means? In verse 23 he says, "I in them and you in me, that they may become perfectly one, so that the world may know that you sent me and loved them even as you loved me." The Father has given us glory (17:22) by sending Jesus—the glorious one—to live within us by his Spirit (17:23). How does this produce unity among us?

Read through the following three sections on *Gospel Glimpses*, *Whole-Bible Connections*, and *Theological Soundings*. Then take time to consider the *Personal Implications* these sections have for you.

Gospel Glimpses

JESUS MEANS FOR HIS PRAYER TO BE OVERHEARD. In John 17 Jesus speaks to the Father. But he also speaks *for* the disciples, because he clearly means them to listen in on his conversation. He prays aloud, near enough and loud enough to be overheard. The reality that he *wants* his disciples to hear his prayer is suggested by two other interactions between Father and Son in John's Gospel. In John 12 God speaks from heaven to Jesus, and Jesus then tells the assembled crowd, "This voice has come for your sake, not mine" (12:30). In John 11 Jesus stands outside the tomb of his friend Lazarus and lifts his eyes to heaven (as he does in 17:1), saying, "Father, I thank you that you have heard me. I knew that you always hear me, but I said this on account of the people standing around, that they may believe that you sent me" (11:41–42). Jesus prays to the Father in such a way that those who overhear will be taught and encouraged. This is good news! Jesus' prayer life is oriented toward helping and encouraging his disciples. We can learn from Jesus. Although our public prayers should never be infected by the fear of people, our public prayers should always intend to edify, encourage, and instruct those who listen.

LOVED BY GOD. Nothing is better than knowing we are loved and cared for by God. The inclusion of John 17 in our Bibles allows the people of God—those who trust in Jesus Christ—to bask in the joy of hearing God's speaking to God about our protection, provision, and unity, all for his glory. This great prayer flows from love (13:1) and expresses Jesus' aim of reproducing love within his followers (17:26). If you have not yet trusted in Jesus Christ, you are warmly welcomed to believe, become part of God's family, and experience his love for you. After all, that is the very purpose for which John's Gospel was written (20:30–31).

Whole-Bible Connections

THE SON OF DESTRUCTION HAS BEEN LOST. Jesus says he has "kept" his disciples in the Father's name during his ministry (17:12). This is the same word that Jesus uses when he asks the Father to "keep" the disciples in his name (17:11) and to "keep" them from the evil one (17:15). Because of Jesus' guarding, "not one of them has been lost except the son of destruction, that the Scripture might be fulfilled" (17:12). Perhaps Jesus is thinking here of what he said earlier about Judas, in John 13:18–19, where he identified Judas's betrayal of him as the fulfillment of Psalm 41:9. The events of Jesus' passion[1] and death are not outside God's control; this is demonstrated by the fact that even the most difficult and painful circumstances fulfill Scripture.

Theological Soundings

GIVEN BY THE FATHER TO THE SON. Jesus' prayer in John 17 reflects the deep commitment of Father and Son to their people. Jesus repeatedly refers to the disciples as those whom the Father has "given" to him (17:2, 6, 9, 24). This recalls what he said earlier in John's Gospel: "All that the Father gives me will come to me" (6:37). Coming to Jesus means believing in him, so Jesus teaches that the Father's work of giving individuals to the Son is the basis of their belief in the Son. In fact, Jesus says, "No one can come to me [i.e., believe in me] unless the Father who sent me draws him" (6:44). So, while we must believe in order to be saved, the only way we can believe is if the Father gives/draws us to Jesus. John 17:6–8 shows that God's giving of the disciples to Jesus is the ground of their belief.

WE BELONG TO THE FATHER. A little detail in this passage is worth treasuring. When the Father gives someone to the Son (17:2, 6, 9, 24), that does not make the person any less the Father's. In verse 9 Jesus says he is praying for those "whom you have given me, for they *are* yours" (present tense). In verse 10 he says to the Father, "All mine are yours, and yours are mine, and I am glorified in them." The people of God belong *simultaneously* to the Father and to the Son.

Personal Implications

Take time to reflect on the implications of John 17:1–26 for your own life today. Make notes below on the personal implications for your walk with the Lord of (1) the *Gospel Glimpses*, (2) the *Whole-Bible Connections*, (3) the *Theological Soundings*, and (4) this passage as a whole.

1. Gospel Glimpses

2. Whole-Bible Connections

3. Theological Soundings

4. John 17:1–26

As You Finish This Unit . . .

Take a moment now to ask for the Lord's blessing and help as you continue in this study of John 13–17. Take a moment also to look back through this unit of study, to reflect on some key things that the Lord may be teaching you, and perhaps to highlight and underline these things to review in the future.

Definitions

[1] **Passion** – The final events of Jesus' life leading up to his death, as recorded in the New Testament Gospels.

Week 12: Summary and Conclusion

In this final study we will step back to ponder and apply what God has shown us through our time in John 13–17. There will be opportunity to review some of your most important reflections from the various *Gospel Glimpses*, *Whole-Bible Connections*, and *Theological Soundings*.

The Big Picture of John 13–17

On the night before his sin-atoning death the loving Jesus prepares his followers and prays for them, fostering a loving community of disciples who will continue his mission to the world.

As we have seen throughout our study, everything Jesus says and does in John 13–17 is in light of his impending death/departure and is motivated by love for "his own," the community (which will include Jew and Gentile) he is gathering around himself. He loves his followers "to the end" (until his death and as much as anyone possibly can). Jesus' love in John 13–17 is not theoretical or hypothetical but real love for real people with real problems—for Peter, who denies him, and for the disciples, who abandon him. And let us ponder once again the reality that these chapters take place *the night before Jesus' death*. We might expect to see how a condemned man tells his friends how they can encourage him, make him more comfortable, or serve him in various ways. Instead, Jesus flips the script. He serves his friends. He washes the disciples' feet, calls them together into a loving community, reassures them of abundant provision after his impending departure, urges them to remain spiritually united to him, warns them of the hatred and persecution they will receive from a hostile world, strengthens their courage through his assurance that he has overcome the world, and then prays to the Father for them. Could Jesus serve his followers any more fully? Yes, he could—and he will. Tomorrow he will die for them. "Greater love has no one than this, that someone lay down his life for his friends" (15:13). The cross is not an aberration in Jesus' life; it is a *continuation and consummation* of it.

First Corinthians 13 contains perhaps the most famous exposition of love in the Bible ("Love is patient and kind; love does not envy or boast; it is not arrogant or rude"; 1 Cor. 13:4–5). Some preachers have suggested that one good way to read 1 Corinthians 13 is to replace the word "love" with the name of Jesus, since Jesus is the perfect embodiment of love. To see love in real life, love in three dimensions, we need only look to him. Love has a face and a name. *Jesus* is patient and kind; *Jesus* does not envy or boast; *Jesus* is not arrogant or rude. John 13–17 is an exquisite portrait of a loving Savior.

Gospel Glimpses

The beautiful gospel of Jesus Christ is present throughout John 13–17. It is there in Jesus' washing of his disciples' feet. We hear it just under the surface in Jesus' ironic question to Peter, "Will you lay down your life for me?" (John 13:38). Its prize is evident in Jesus' description of the many rooms of his Father's house (14:2), and its pain is felt as Jesus grows troubled in his spirit (13:21). Jesus' death will take away the sin of the world (1:29). It will be the moment of his greatest agony and simultaneously the greatest revelation of his glory (17:1–5).

How has this study of John 13–17 brought new clarity to your understanding of the gospel?

What particular passages or themes in John 13–17 have led you to a fresh grasp of God's grace through Jesus?

Whole-Bible Connections

John 13–17 is not understandable apart from the larger storyline of the whole Bible. Jesus' imminent death, as well as the hostility of the world toward his disciples and the ultimate hope Jesus offers them, makes sense only within the Bible's framework of Creation/Fall/Redemption/New Creation. Moreover, as we have seen, these chapters form Jesus' Farewell Discourse, a genre that was widely known in the Old Testament and Jewish literature. Of course, the unique feature of this particular Farewell Discourse is that the man about to die will not remain dead! He will rise on the third day (John 20). Throughout our study we have seen that the events leading to Jesus' death fulfill the Scriptures (13:18; 15:25), that Jesus himself perfects and fulfills the Old Testament role of Israel (John 15:1), and that Jesus' promises to his disciples are the fulfillment of Old Testament expectations (16:7–15).

How has your understanding of the place of John 13–17 in the broader sweep of the Bible been deepened through this study?

What are some connections between John 13–17 and the Old Testament that you had not noticed before? What are some New Testament connections that you had not previously seen?

Are there any themes emphasized in John 13–17 that have helped deepen your grasp of the Bible's unity? Which one(s)?

Because John 13–17 is just one part of John's Gospel we have regularly read these chapters in light of John's larger story. If you have never studied the entirety of John's Gospel, you may consider doing so, using the *Knowing the Bible* study guide for the Gospel of John.

Theological Soundings

John 13–17 has much to contribute to Christian theology. While it contains important teaching on God the Father, the person and work of the Holy Spirit ("the Helper"), and the formation of Jesus' new community of followers, perhaps its most important contribution is what it teaches about Christ. The deity of Jesus is on full display in this Gospel. Jesus has existed from eternity past (13:3; 16:28) in divine glory (17:5), loved by the Father (17:24). To see him is to see the Father (14:9). His followers are to believe in God and believe in him (14:1). His comprehensive foreknowledge of his death demonstrates his deity (13:19). Although Satan and Judas are active in pursuing the crucifixion for their own nefarious purposes (13:2, 27), neither can force it to occur (14:30–31). Jesus lays down his own life freely (10:17–18; 14:30–31), and he sovereignly directs events (13:27). And yet, while Jesus' deity is highlighted, his humility and humanity are also clear to see. He does the work of a slave, washing his disciples' feet. He prioritizes their needs even as he prepares to die for them. He is "troubled in his spirit" (13:21). The stunning truth John's Gospel teaches is that Jesus' glory and Jesus' humility in fact belong closely together. It is at the very moment of his greatest humiliation, as he hangs on the cross dying for sin, that he is supremely glorified with divine glory (13:31–32; 17:5; cf. 12:23, 27–28, 32–33).

In what ways has your theology been corrected, shaped, deepened, or improved through this study of John 13–17?

How would our understanding of God be diminished if John 13–17 were not in the Bible?

Personal Implications

There is nothing more powerfully life-changing than knowing that Christ loves *you* specifically. Not just people in general, but *you*. The apostle Paul never got over this knowledge (Rom. 8:35; Gal. 2:20). In fact, Christ's love for him became his driving motivation in all of life. He said that it "controlled" him (2 Cor. 5:14–15).

How has your study of John 13–17 increased your awareness of the loving heart of Christ? Have you personally experienced his love for *you* in the course of this study? Are there steps you can take to put yourself in a position to receive and enjoy the love of Christ more regularly? If so, what are they?

What other aspects of Jesus' character have you seen and celebrated in John 13–17? How will you pray and live differently in light of what you have seen of your Savior?

As we have observed, Jesus does more in John 13–17 than love others. He also fosters a *community* of people who love—the church. He does this not only by commanding love but by transforming individual lives through an experience of his love (13:34; 17:23, 26). This mutual love is to be the distinguishing feature of Jesus' followers (13:35). It may often look mundane: providing childcare for a weary young mother, showing up to your small group each week, praying faithfully for a fellow Christian struggling with addiction. But it is actually glorious, because it glorifies God (15:8). When Jesus' followers pursue love for one another, we are doing that which Jesus commanded the church to do, and we are pointing people to Jesus himself.

Are you part of a church family that is living out Jesus' call to love one another? What are some ways in which God may be inviting you to grow in receiving love from other Christians and extending it to them?

Recall one of the significant themes of our study: Throughout John 13–17 Jesus is preparing and empowering his followers for effective gospel witness to a hostile world. And it turns out that he was successful! The church witnessed to the beauty of Christ even when it cost God's people their lives. The gospel was passed along, generation by generation, and eventually it came to you. How might God be using this study of John 13–17 to prepare and empower you for faithful gospel witness?

As You Finish Studying Jesus' Farewell Discourse . . .

We rejoice with you as you complete this study of John 13–17! Take a moment now to ask for the Lord to use what you have studied for his glory and your good. May you be more in awe of the greatness of Jesus, more open to receiving his overflowing love for you, and more deeply united to the vine as you bear the good fruit of abiding in him. May his words remain in you, and may you be faithfully consistent in studying the Word of God. To continue your study of the Bible, we would encourage you to consider other books in the *Knowing the Bible* series, and to visit www.crossway.org/knowingthebible.

Be encouraged to review this study from time to time. Revisit the notes you have written and the things you have highlighted or underlined. Reflect again on the key themes that the Lord has been teaching you about himself and about his Word. May your joy be full (John 15:11; 16:24; 17:13).

KNOWING THE BIBLE STUDY GUIDE SERIES

Experience the *Grace* of God in the *Word* of God

Series Volumes

- Genesis
- Exodus
- Leviticus
- Numbers
- Deuteronomy
- Joshua
- Judges
- Ruth and Esther
- 1–2 Samuel
- 1–2 Kings
- 1–2 Chronicles
- Ezra and Nehemiah
- Job
- Psalms
- Proverbs
- Ecclesiastes
- Song of Solomon
- Isaiah
- Jeremiah
- Lamentations, Habakkuk, and Zephaniah
- Ezekiel
- Daniel
- Hosea
- Joel, Amos, and Obadiah
- Jonah, Micah, and Nahum
- Haggai, Zechariah, and Malachi
- Matthew
- Mark
- Luke
- John
- Acts
- Romans
- 1 Corinthians
- 2 Corinthians
- Galatians
- Ephesians
- Philippians
- Colossians and Philemon
- 1–2 Thessalonians
- 1–2 Timothy and Titus
- Hebrews
- James
- 1–2 Peter and Jude
- 1–3 John
- Revelation
- The Parables of Jesus
- The Sermon on the Mount
- The Ten Commandments
- Jesus' Farewell Discourse
- Jesus' Speech on the Mount of Olives
- The Miracles of Jesus

crossway.org/knowingthebible